KANTHA

KANTHA

Sustainable Textiles
and Mindful Making

Ekta Kaul

HERBERT PRESS
LONDON • OXFORD • NEW YORK • NEW DELHI • SYDNEY

HERBERT PRESS
Bloomsbury Publishing Plc
50 Bedford Square, London, WC1B 3DP, UK
Bloomsbury Publishing Ireland Limited
29 Earlsfort Terrace, Dublin 2, D02 AY28, Ireland

BLOOMSBURY, HERBERT PRESS and the Herbert Press logo are
trademarks of Bloomsbury Publishing Plc

First published in Great Britain in 2024

A catalogue record for this book is available from the British Library
Library of Congress Cataloguing-in-Publication data has been applied for

ISBN: HB: 978 1 7899-4043-5; eBook· 978-1-7899-4041-1

2 4 6 8 10 9 7 5 3

Designed and typeset by Tina Hobson
Printed and bound in Turkey by Elma Basim

CONVERSION CHART

Metric		Imperial
2.5 centimetres (cm)	=	1 inch (in)
90 centimetres	=	1 yard (yd)
1 metre (m)	=	39 inches

To find out more about our authors and books visit **www.bloomsbury.com**
and sign up for our newsletters

For product safety related questions contact **productsafety@bloomsbury.com**

For

my mother, Sucheta, who taught me the art of stitch
and
my father, Krishan, who instilled in me a love of storytelling

Contents

Foreword   7
Introduction   8

Kantha Tradition   *18*
Kantha Taxonomy   *30*
Stitch Techniques   *40*
Construction   *110*
Reimagining Tradition   *124*
Creating Your Own Kantha   *170*

Conclusion   *187*
Suppliers   *188*
Acknowledgements   *189*
Picture Credits   *190*
Bibliography   *191*
Index of Stitch Techniques   *192*

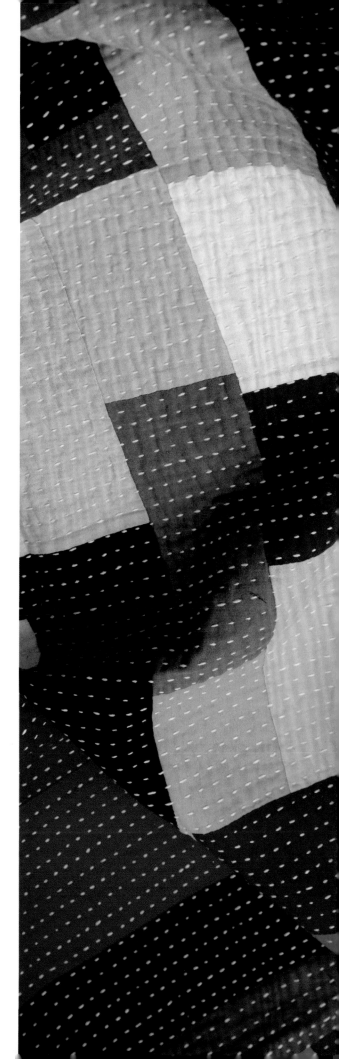

Foreword

Katie Treggiden

Founder and director of *Making Design Circular*

I bundled out of the Tube station, dashed across the road, and made my way into the converted church. I stopped to catch my breath before tackling the stairs. At the top was a tiny room tucked into the bell tower, where I was immediately greeted by Ekta Kaul. A group of women sat around a long piece of fabric onto which Ekta had hand-drawn a map, and each of them was embroidering a different part of it. Ekta gave me a needle, thread and some basic instructions, and the strangest thing happened – as I started to sew, I felt my heart rate slow, my breath deepen and my hands steady. I had recently been diagnosed with anxiety and I remember telling Ekta afterwards that it was the first time I had felt calm in months.

I left school proud of the fact I 'couldn't sew' (despite an A* in GCSE textiles). To my young mind, feminism meant emulating men. I wanted to be an author and a journalist – I didn't have time to be anybody's housewife. So, I put down my needle and thread. This book is an important reminder of why I was wrong.

Sewing in the company of other women is an ancient practice that has proven mental health benefits, as I experienced first-hand in that belfry tower. But Ekta's telling of the story of kantha reveals that it is also so much more. Kantha gave women the opportunity, not only

to earn, but also to capture the multifaceted female experience in a sophisticated visual and tactile language that drew on – and at times subverted – religion and politics, domestic life and the natural world. Kantha provides evidence that women have forever been, not just lovers, wives and mothers, but documenters and critics of the times in which they lived. And yet, until 1800, no-one thought kantha were valuable enough to keep. The potential for a nuanced experience of womanhood has been so supressed that, almost two centuries later, I still thought I had to choose between so-called 'women's work' and having a voice.

In this book, Ekta has collected fragments of stories – some worn, some forgotten and some purposely erased – and stitched them back together to create something powerful. The word 'history' also reads 'his story', and the male perspective and/or gaze dominates books about craft and design. *Kantha: Sustainable Textiles and Mindful Making* is an attempt to put that right. Ekta describes kantha as a 'restitution of wholeness', and her book is exactly that. In fact, it could be described as a work of kantha in itself – a palimpsest of meaning, carefully re-constructed with love. And I for one am grateful for it.

Introduction

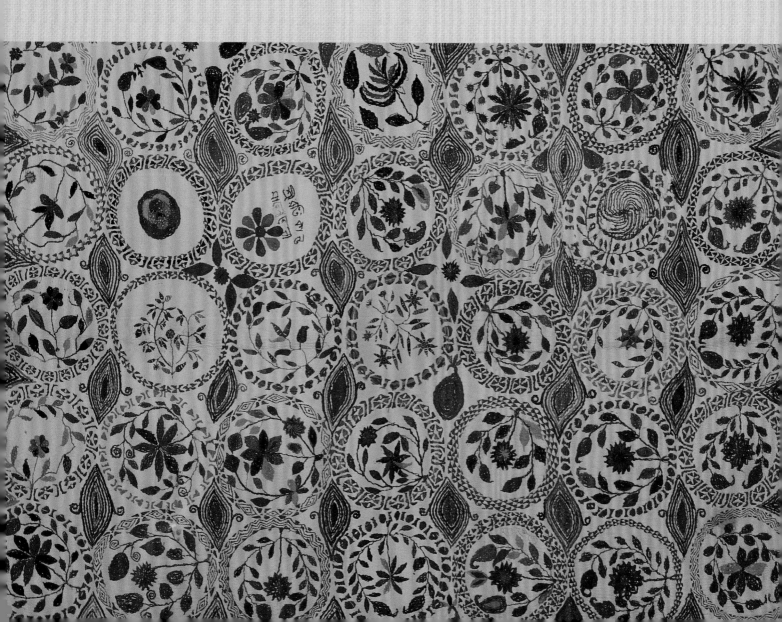

Kantha – Layers of Meaning

Cloth and embroidery form the patchwork of my earliest childhood memories. My mother, a prolific embroiderer, often told stories about Nani – my maternal grandmother – who grew up in Kolkata, Bengal and who loved to embroider. Although I never met her in person, since she had passed away long before my birth, I got to know her through her stitches. I learnt of her love of nature from a small framed embroidery that hung on my parents' bedroom wall when I was little – two sparrows sitting on a branch – that Nani had embroidered in incredibly minute, meticulous stitches. By observing the way my mother kept Nani's half-finished embroidery of a yellow urn amongst her most precious possessions, wrapped tenderly in a diaphanous *mulmul*, I learnt of the power of stitch to comfort and soothe and its potent ability to be a conduit for connection across space and time. Studying the handful of sepia-toned photographs of Nani that we had at home, I imagined her graceful figure wearing the handwoven gossamer-thin Bengali saris that my mother had inherited from her. I caught fleeting glimpses of Nani's life in the stories I heard of her childhood in Kolkata and the intriguing narrative of the family's considerable fortune in the jute trade, which was significantly impacted by Bengal's partition in 1947. The partition caused the overnight separation of jute fields and factories across borders, causing a rupture in communities and livelihoods, and ultimately led to the family's move to North India.

My grandmother passed on when my mother was still a child and many stories were lost in the intervening decades, but what stayed with my mother was a love of embroidery and Bengali textiles, I suspect as comforting reminders of her maternal heritage. Kantha, baluchari and jamdani saris from Bengal remained a beloved part of my mother's

wardrobe. In my childhood home, the rituals of wearing and caring for saris punctuated the seasons – my mother's monochrome kantha saris, with their distinctive black embroidery on ecru tussar silk, heralded winters; the starching of her cotton saris and the putting away of the kantha in neat piles, with neem leaves in their folds, announced the arrival of spring; the soothing tones of her cotton jamdani saris welcomed the summer.

▲ I got to know Leela, my maternal grandmother, through her embroidery and her Bengali saris. She is standing to the right.

The love of stitch was all around me while I was growing up. My mother taught me to embroider and I learnt quiltmaking from my paternal grandmother, who introduced me to the practice of stitching quilts using layers of cast-off cloth. She stitched *gudris*, layering fragments of fabrics with lengths of worn-out saris, quilting them together with simple running stitches. My interest in textiles grew steadily, and turned into a deep love of the medium as I studied Apparel & Textile Design at the National Institute of Design, Ahmedabad. As a design student I learnt about the rich textile traditions of India, including kantha embroidery.

Spurred by a desire to explore textiles in more depth, I moved to the UK to undertake a master's degree and, after graduating, established my artistic practice here. In the pursuit of my own artistic voice, I turned to running stitch, drawn by its profound simplicity as a mark and my innate affinity to its vocabulary, quite possibly because of its associations with home. This affinity led me to study the history of the running stitch and its forms in different cultures. I learnt about the Japanese *boro* tradition and returned again to the Indian kantha tradition. Connecting with kantha again after so many years, while living thousands of miles away from India, brought me closer to my Indian heritage, my mother and grandmothers. I discovered a whole universe of meaning behind the stitches.

From being domestic artefacts that document personal narratives through the feminine perspective, to being symbols of love passed down the generations, to being prime examples of sustainable design, kantha contain layers of significance. The visual and tactile vocabulary of kantha is not only inspirational in its own right, but also carries powerful ideas of identity, tradition, comfort, storytelling, heritage, self-expression, mindful making and sustainability, all of which I find deeply inspiring. As an artist I am drawn to kantha's expansive capacity to hold a multitude of meanings all at once. This book seeks to unravel the multi-layered meanings that kantha embody, with the hope that they may inspire you to adopt them in your own practice.

Kantha refers to embroidered, unwadded quilts made with layers of discarded fabric made primarily in West Bengal (India) and Bangladesh in the Indian subcontinent. The word 'kantha' is believed to have originated from the Sanskrit word 'kontha', meaning rags. Traditionally, Bengali women embroidered kantha by layering cast-off saris and dhotis to create richly decorated textiles as testaments of love, celebratory documents of rites of passage and archives of self-expression. They incorporated narratives and motifs from their daily lives, folklore, religious beliefs, flora, fauna, and their hopes and wishes.

Threads unravelled from sari borders were used to create intricate illustrative or abstract patterns employing a rich vocabulary of stitches, including running stitch, pattern darning, back stitch and many more. Of these stitches, running stitch and its variations were by far the most popular. Kantha tradition continues to evolve, and today kantha can be seen in multiple avatars – quilts, saris, bags, scarves, pillows, bedspreads and wall art. The term 'kantha' has come to encompass both the objects and the running stitch used to create them.

Kantha, with its embodiment of sustainability, mindfulness and self-expression, provides a vital solution to the challenges we face in the post-pandemic world, including high stress levels, the desire for a slower pace of life and the urgent need to address climate change. The historical and contemporary kantha approaches presented in this book aim to invite you to adopt a more sustainable and mindful way of making, and to use stitch to express your unique way of seeing the world. It is my hope that these starting points will serve as catalysts for developing your practice further.

▶ My mother's
black and ecru
kantha (*left*) and
diaphanous jamdani
(*right*) saris were my
first introduction
to Bengali textile
traditions.

Art by Women

▲ Kantha. Courtesy of Crafts Council of West Bengal, Artisana store, Kolkata.

Traditionally, women used the canvas of kantha to embroider their lived experiences, leaving behind a rich account of their lives in stitches. Within an underlying structure marked by grids, borders and motifs or patterns arranged symmetrically, the women exercised artistic freedom to express themselves through motifs that reflected the world they lived in, their interests, ideas, fears, hopes and desires. On kantha, women employed technical skills in needlework, which were learnt and refined over generations to make their interiority visible, to create receptacles of beauty and to hold space for their own personal narratives. Pika Ghosh describes making kantha as 'the visualisation of

a process of interiorisation' in her book *Making Kantha, Making Home*.

Women created kantha in a multitude of sizes to mark rites of passage of loved ones, forge familial alliances, strengthen bonds, assert their views and simply add beauty to the everyday. Stella Kramrisch highlights the link between traditional kantha making and the *vrata* (a tradition of fasting for a blessing or as an offering of gratitude to the gods) and *alpona* (rice paste ritualistic drawings made by women on the floor to protect the family). Many *alpona* patterns and kantha motifs hold striking similarities.

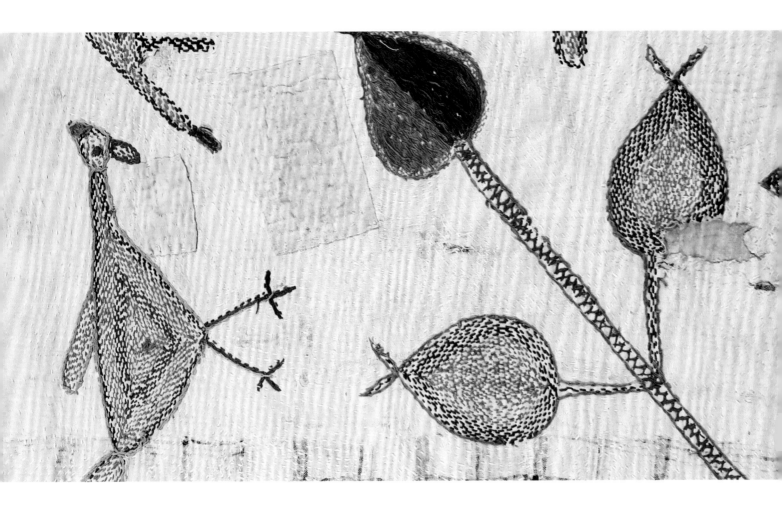

The Original Circular Design

Historically, kantha quilts were created using worn-out saris that were no longer usable, stitched with threads drawn from the borders of saris. Kantha were regularly mended; tears were patched and stitched with remnants of fabric from the household or fragments of other kantha. They were recycled into smaller objects like coin purses, patches for other kantha, diapers and cleaning rags until the fabric fell apart completely, and could no longer be used.

This practice of reincarnating the old into the new was not just rooted in thrift and preservation, but also in the spirit of making whole, avoiding waste and a deep respect for materials, which permeates the Indian way of life. The women who made kantha were incorporating sustainable practices in everyday life well before such practices became part of a mainstream discourse on sustainability. And yet, until recently, kantha making or the women's contribution was simply not acknowledged in popular discourses on sustainability, despite the fact that they are embodiments of circular design. This book attempts to highlight this undercelebrated aspect of kantha and its unsung heroines.

▲ Adding patches of fabric is a popular mending technique in kantha in order to extend its life. Here raw edges of the patch are turned over and hemmed on to the ground cloth, possibly to cover a torn section, or to strengthen a worn-out section. This is followed by quilting using a similar stitch size and thread as the base. Sometimes scraps of old kantha are also used as patches. Collection of the National Crafts Museum, New Delhi.

Kantha's Emotional DNA

At its heart, kantha is a symbol of love – a carrier of blessings and hopes from the maker to the receiver, often from mother to daughter, but also across generations, families and community. Layers of cloth that once wrapped family members are used in kantha, and their touch evokes memories of the comfort of home and of loved ones. Pika Ghosh in *Making Kantha, Making Home* describes kantha as 'transmitters of touch'.

During my research, I spoke with makers, users and collectors of kantha: curators, researchers, revivalists, gallerists, artists, designers and artisans, as well as those who make kantha for their family members in Kolkata, Delhi, Bengaluru, Ahmedabad and London. A common thread of comfort, home

and the ability of kantha to hold memories and express emotions runs through all their accounts.

When I interviewed Bappaditya Biswas – co-founder of Byloom, a Kolkata-based store specialising in Indian fabrics and clothing – about his personal relationship with kantha, he warmly reminisced about his grandmother asking him which design he would prefer on his kantha and then proceeding to stitch his favourite motifs onto his quilt. Decades later, he still holds on to this treasure. Artist Bhasha Chakrabarti, who lives in the USA, uses kantha in her practice to explore ideas of her identity. As you will see in the following chapters, kantha continues to inspire creative expressions across the world.

▲ Kantha for swaddling a baby, probably early eighteenth century, from Faridpur, East Bengal (present-day Bangladesh), 76 × 76cm (30 × 30in). From the collection of Prof. Aloke Kumar, Kolkata.

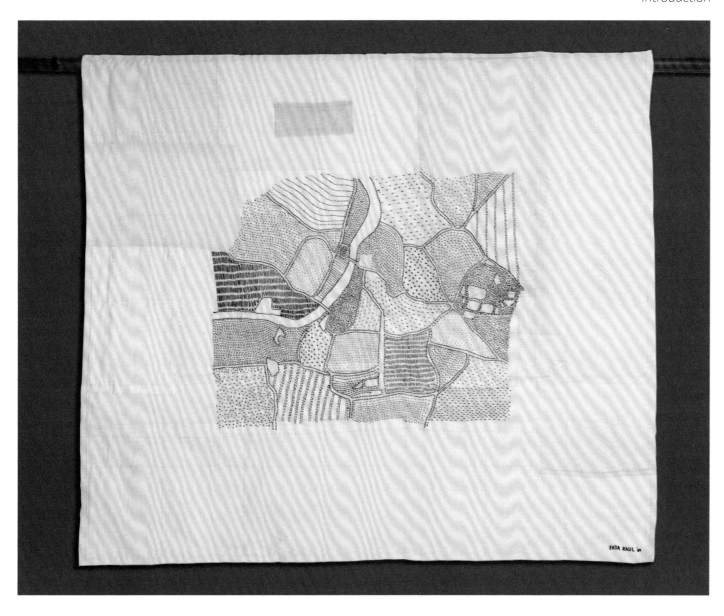

▲ Ekta Kaul,
Threads of Connection
(2022), 106 × 90cm
(42 × 35in).
Commissioned by
TOAST.

Threads of Connection

Threads of Connection explores my search for my maternal grandmother, who grew up in Kolkata and who sadly I never met. When I visited Kolkata to carry out fieldwork for this book, I took the opportunity to look for her. However, with not much to go on other than a street name where she lived nearly eighty years ago, my search proved futile. In response, I embroidered this work in kantha-inspired stitches, mapping Kolkata and the neighbourhoods my grandmother would have known. As I stitched the contours of the Hooghly, I imagined her walking by the river and felt our connection renewed once again.

Kantha, which originates in Bengal and gives a new life to old cloth, seemed like a fitting way to honour our lost, but perhaps rekindled, connection. I created the ground cloth by layering remnant fabrics from my studio and recycled scraps from my wardrobe, joining them with offcuts from the studio of lifestyle brand TOAST, who commissioned this piece for Eternally Yours, an exhibition exploring ideas of care, repair and healing at Somerset House, London (June–September 2022). Joining the fragments together became a metaphor for my fragmented family history, and embroidering them with narrative stitch became an act of healing for me. A portion of the map remains blank as a poignant but hopeful reminder that a part of her story is still missing, and I might yet find the missing piece.

Documents of Meditation

One of the many reasons I choose to embroider is to nurture a connection with my inner world. Stitch becomes a segue to a place of solace, comfort and equanimity, especially in the midst of balancing demands of motherhood, artmaking and a busy studio practice. My mother embroidered prolifically, often sitting down with her threads and needle at the end of a busy day at work, (I suspect) as a reprieve from the rigours of academia. It is not hard to imagine that Bengali women also experienced the same sense of calm through kantha stitch.

Riverside Walk

Walks by the Thames and stitching are my meditative rituals. Both are transitions for me into quiet contemplation and inspiration – an intentional calibration on my part to return to harmony. This work maps my walks and expresses the sense of tranquillity I feel being surrounded by nature. In our fast-paced twenty-first-century lives, moments of being still are few and far between. However, taking inspiration from kantha, we can build these moments into our lives through intentional stitch practice.

One of the many reasons I choose to embroider is to nurture a connection with my inner world.

▲ Ekta Kaul, *Riverside Walk* (2022), 50 × 50cm (20 × 20in).

Kantha as Empowerment

Today kantha supports the livelihoods of thousands of women artisans, not just in Bengal and Bangladesh but also across India, responding to the growing demand from collectors and connoisseurs globally. In the rural milieu of the subcontinent, where women continue to face significant restrictions to access to education and social mobility, kantha provides an invaluable means to economic independence and empowerment. In India, a growing ecosystem of non-governmental organisations (NGOs) such as SHE Kantha, SASHA and Street Survivors India, plus contemporary designers, ateliers, sustainability-led lifestyle brands and conscious consumers, is engaged in reviving and revitalising kantha and supporting livelihoods of the kantha makers. Shabnam Ramaswamy is the founder of Street Survivors

India, a craft cooperative of over 1,500 women engaged in kantha making in Katna and nearby villages in Murshidabad, West Bengal. She notes that 'having their own source of income not only makes the women financially independent but also gives them a voice, to some extent, within a conservative and patriarchal society.'

While the traditional domestic practice of making kantha still continues, institutionalised production of kantha in response to market demands from cosmopolitan consumers in India and globally has brought in significant changes – for instance, the adoption of predetermined designs and colour schemes, the use of new instead of worn-out fabrics and the shift from multiple layers to a single layer. Unlike in the past, the use of embroidery frames instead of freehand embroidery is also now common.

▼ Street Survivors India members wearing their kantha creations.

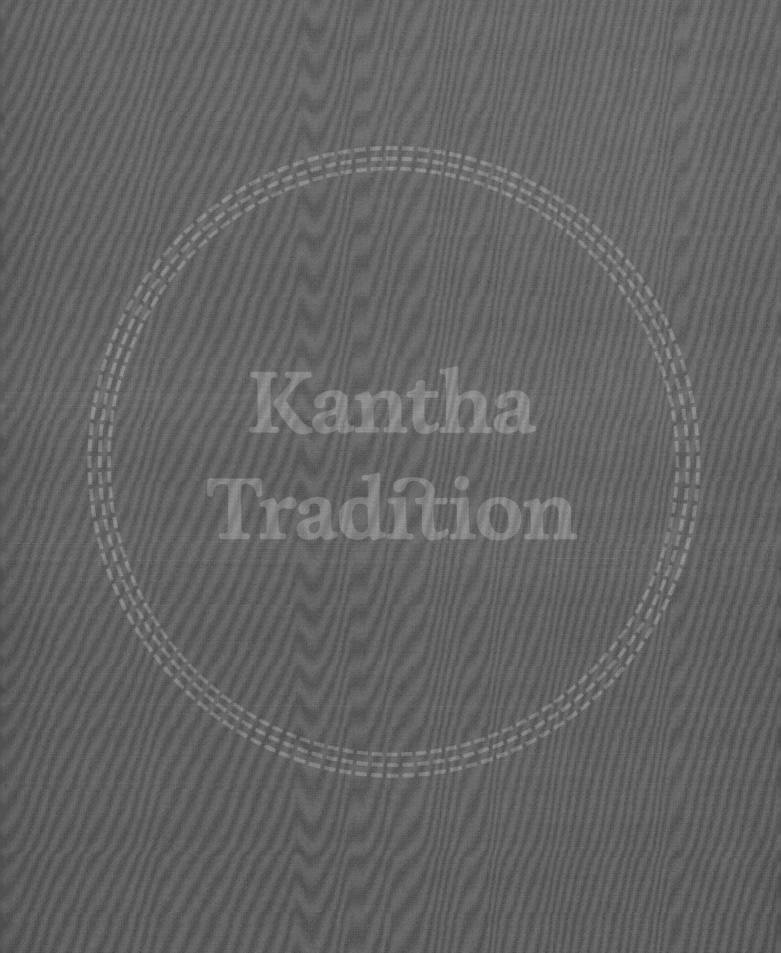

Kantha
Tradition

Bengal

Bengal is an historical region in the eastern part of the Indian subcontinent, located to the north of the Bay of Bengal, consisting of present-day Bangladesh and West Bengal (India). The area encompasses a shared culture, rooted in centuries-old common linguistic and historical traditions that continue to this day, despite the traumatic partition of the region in 1947 into East Pakistan (now Bangladesh) and West Bengal (India) by the then British colonial administration. This chapter refers to Bengal as a pre-partition whole.

The name Bengal is said to be derived from the ancient kingdom of Banga, as recorded in the Indian epic *Mahabharata* in the first millennium BCE. The region's history stretches back even further to Neolithic times and early rice-growing communities. The Ganga, Brahmaputra and Meghna rivers, along with their various distributaries, make the Bengal delta one of the most fertile regions in the Indian subcontinent. Agriculture is the predominant occupation, even today. The weather is hot and humid for most of the year, punctuated by monsoons and mild winters. Travelling through rural West Bengal, I was struck by the similarities between rows of kantha stitches with their textured ridges and the rows of paddy saplings in the fields with their textures on the landscape.

▶ (*Top*) Paddy fields in West Bengal.

▶ Khejur or Indian date (*Phoenix sylvestris*) grow abundantly in the region. In the past, thorns of the tree were used for tacking layers of fabric together as a method of stabilising the fabrics before beginning kantha embroidery.

Throughout history, Bengal was a lucrative destination for invaders, merchants and colonists. Sultans, Mughals, the Portuguese, Dutch and British were all drawn to the region because of its fertile lands, which produced an abundance of rice, jute and indigo; its exquisite muslins and fine textiles; and its prosperity as a thriving entrepôt with extensive global maritime connections. Waves of traders and conquerors from different parts of the world, and skilled artisans, artists and merchants from other regions of India, settled in Bengal, bringing with them their languages, subcultures and practices. This unique blend of diverse influences has shaped the culture of Bengal, resulting in a rich tapestry of pluralism, which is reflected in its cuisine, language, textiles and material culture.

Waves of traders and conquerors from different parts of the world, and skilled artisans, artists and merchants from other regions of India, settled in Bengal.

▲ Train station at Bolpur Santiniketan, painted in vibrant colours. I was struck by the Mughal influence on the architecture, especially the tiered pillars, arched doorways and floral patterns decorating them.

Textile Heritage

Bengal has a rich textile heritage, and has been famed for its superlative cottons since antiquity. Roman records show that Bengali muslins were the most sought-after luxury goods in the ancient world, as explored by Enamul Haque in *Woven Air*. He further notes that detailed descriptions of textiles in the *Arthashastra* – an ancient Indian treatise on statecraft written in the third century BCE – reveal a well-established textile industry serving vast domestic and international markets. Muslins 'so fine that multiple yards could pass through a ring' were handwoven in Dhaka, the capital of present-day Bangladesh.

Dhakai muslin, as it was referred to, was handspun and woven with a rare cotton that only grew along the banks of the Meghna River. Muslin production flourished during the Mughal era (sixteenth to seventeenth centuries); however, the fabric's global patronage is said to stretch back thousands of years, with ancient Greeks among its earliest known patrons. Multiple varieties of muslin were developed and became renowned for their diaphanous beauty and poetic names such as *abrawan* (running water), *shabnam* (evening dew), *bafthana* (woven air) and *mulmul khas* (emperor's special muslin) in the Mughal court, as Haque notes. Bengali muslins were coveted across Europe and Asia, resulting in a prosperous export industry. However, the art of spinning and weaving these extraordinary muslins was sadly lost due to colonisation and the subsequent flooding of Indian markets with industrially produced, British-made textile goods. Efforts to revive the traditional fine muslins have gained momentum in the last few decades.

Other distinctive textile traditions from the region include jamdani (exquisitely woven fine cottons with an intricate supplementary weft technique, akin to embroidery on the loom) and baluchari (saris woven with narrative scenes from Indian epics *Mahabharata* and *Ramayana*). Both these heritage textiles continue to be handwoven today and are worn as saris or used as yardage for home and fashion accessories. It is interesting to note the synergetic relationship of embroidery and weaving in Bengali textiles. The needlework in kantha meticulously replicates woven sari borders, while the shuttle moves in and out of warp threads in jamdani to create motifs that emulate needlework.

In the sixteenth and seventeenth centuries, intricately embroidered quilted textiles, referred to as Colcha (Portuguese for bedcover), were embroidered in the Satgaon region of Bengal for Portuguese, and later for English aristocratic patrons and collectors. Skilled artisans created luxurious bedspreads, altar pieces and wall panels with intricate designs that typically depicted classical, biblical and Hindu iconography, floral patterns and animal figures arranged in successive concentric panels, and grids around a central panel with distinct bands at the borders. Embroidery was predominantly worked in minute chain stitch using a cream wild silk, usually tussar, eri or muga, on a white cotton ground, although Colcha embroidered on other base-cloth colours, such as indigo, are also known. The Colcha displayed at the Victoria & Albert Museum in London and the Museu Nacional de Arte Antiga in Lisbon are excellent examples of this transcultural marine trade. Colcha quilts share a close visual relationship with kantha, with a similar layout of design elements incorporating grids, a central medallion and borders, as explored by John Irwin (Keeper at the Victoria & Albert Museum) and Pika Ghosh in their scholarship.

Kantha Tradition

Historically, textile production for trade was a male-dominated domain. Professional male weavers, dyers, printers and embroiderers were employed in workshops or worked as independent artisans. As textiles created exclusively by women, kantha occupy a unique place in the region's fabric heritage. Using layers of discarded cloth – often inherited from family members – and threads unravelled from old sari borders, Bengali women embroidered narratives of their lives on kantha.

Like the varied layers that they comprised, kantha were receptacles of multiple meanings and uses. They served both as practical domestic objects, such as wraps or bedspreads, and cherished heirlooms given to mark significant milestones and rites of passage or as expressions of love. Grandmothers and mothers crafted them for their daughters' trousseau or to celebrate the birth of a child in the family, embroidering the kantha with symbols of blessings and abundance, sometimes even verses. Kantha occupied intimate domestic spaces, they soothed and held its users in their folds, embodying home, touch and connection. They travelled between homes, villages and even nations, and expressed, reaffirmed and negotiated familial and social relationships. Ultimately, kantha are versatile artefacts that hold deep cultural and emotional significance, as highlighted by Pika Ghosh.

Kantha occupied intimate domestic spaces, they soothed and held its users in their folds, embodying home, touch and connection.

The designs found in kantha were reflections of women's lived experiences; their perceptions of contemporary events, mythology or religion; and an expression of their interiority, meditations and contemplations. The subjects they chose to embroider and the placement of motifs, scale, colours, composition, selection of threads and stitch type, reflect the embroiderers' personal discernment and intentional curation, documenting their aesthetic and intellectual choices on cloth. Thus, a single kantha could simultaneously convey a multitude of complex themes, ranging from nature to the domestic, the political and the subversive, capturing the nuanced and multifaceted essence of human experience.

Traditionally, certain conventions were followed for designing and making kantha, for example the use of a lotus blossom (*padma*) as the central motif (*mandal*) symbolising the universe; distinctive stitched borders to mark off edges; and the positioning of paisleys (*kalka*) or trees of life (*jiban brikha*) in the corners. The field of the kantha was then embellished with iconography drawn from nature, folklore, everyday objects, rituals, current events and personal histories around the central *mandal*; the ground was covered with small running stitches (kantha *phor*) joining all the layers by working around the contour motifs in concentric rows, emulating waves, as explained by Mohammad Sayeedur Rahman in *Woven Air*. The central lotus was represented as an eight-petalled, hundred-petalled or even thousand-petalled blossom. While the motifs and borders were embroidered in colour, the stitched ground – representing water that the central lotus rests on – was embroidered in white or cream to match the base cloth, so it read as a texture rather than a pattern, reflecting the embroiderers' sophisticated visual and tactile language. Additionally, the use of grids and

placement of motifs within the grid sections as compositional devices was popular in designing kantha. As most kantha were placed on surfaces horizontally and viewed from above, directional motifs were placed such that they could be viewed the right way up from every side.

The rich diversity in the kantha iconography reflects Bengal's multilayered history and regional differences in the forms of expression as well as the purpose of the kantha. For instance, a fish – symbolising fertility – was embroidered on a kantha intended as a daughter's bridal gift, along with other symbols of abundance and protection, while a *mahrab* – indicating the direction of Mecca

– was stitched on a prayer kantha. Motifs and patterns in the body and the borders (*pars*) expressed a range of meanings, representing everyday objects or the maker's wishes for the user. For instance *prodeep shilai* represents a row of lamps, *dhaner chori* (rice stalks) expresses wishes for abundance, while *chokh par* (eyes) ward off the evil eye. Kantha motifs bear a striking resemblance to *alpona*, the ritualistic floor drawings by women made with rice paste, expressing prayers and vows. Some kantha were also made as part of *vrata*, the practice of abstinence of food, or fasting, as part of a pious observance seeking blessings for a loved one, as explored by Stella Kramrisch.

▲ *Alpona* outside a doorway in Kolkata, made using paint instead of the traditional rice flour (the latter is ephemeral).

◀ The fish is a popular motif in kantha iconography. Collection of the National Craft Museum, New Delhi.

▶ Diversity of styles in embroidering the central lotus *mandal*. Collection of the National Craft Museum, New Delhi.

According to Mohammad Sayeedur Rahman in *Woven Air*, work was begun on auspicious days – Tuesdays for Hindus and Fridays for Muslims; if a pregnant woman began embroidering a kantha for her unborn child and it died, the kantha was given away to a saint and was not used by the family. Upon the arrival of a new bride and her trousseau kantha, a lively exchange of motifs and stitch techniques ensued among the women in the family and the neighbourhood. Proficiency in embroidery elicited pride in the maker and admiration from the community. When kantha travelled from one household to another, designs and ideas spread organically.

As Rituparna Basu discusses in 'The History of Kantha Art', the earliest written reference to kantha is found in Krishnaraj Kaviraj Goswami's biography, *Chaitanya Charitamrita* (1557), detailing the life and teachings of the mystic and saint Chaitanya Mahaprabhu. Oral

traditions and songs, however, suggest kantha making is much older than that.

Traditional kantha provide us with glimpses into women's lives, hopes and aspirations at a certain point in history. Kantha are not only tangible records of lived experiences of women, but also testaments of their creativity and ingenuity. The kantha embroiderers were pioneers in sustainability, reusing tatters to create objects of beauty and expressing themselves with threads drawn from old sari borders. They used stitch to record their points of view, ideas and thoughts. In an era when their choices and opportunities were limited, these creative women demonstrated not only their ethos of recycling and care through their choice of materials and motifs, but also their agency by proving that creativity can thrive despite constraints such as social structures and no access to other art materials or formal training.

Recycling and Restitution

Bengali men and women wore lengths of handwoven cottons and silks draped around the body. Men wore dhotis or lungis (lower garments, pleated and draped around the waist) and women wore saris. The style of draping and the weight of the fabric signified status and identity. Handwoven cottons ranged from coarse to extremely fine and were chosen depending upon the season, and the occupation and economic circumstances of the wearer.

When the clothes became too tattered to be worn and were discarded, Bengali women saved them until they had a sufficient amount for making kantha. Then they layered and stitched the discarded saris, dhotis, lungis and scraps into exquisitely embroidered kantha using the language of narrative stitch. The kantha were cared for and mended by the women, and passed down the generations as an heirloom or given between families as a gift. When a quilt became too fragile to be used, it was turned into smaller functional objects like coin purses or patches and used until it fell apart entirely. Stella Kramrisch describes the material symbolism of kantha with its scraps brought together by stitching 'a restitution of wholeness'.

When the quilt became too fragile to be used, it was turned into smaller functional objects like coin purses or patches and used until it fell apart entirely.

▶ Kantha embroidered in vibrant colours on a white quilted base and embellished with bright blue borders. Courtesy of Street Survivors India, Katna, Murshidabad.

▶ (*Opposite*) A building in present-day Kolkata.

Traditional Kantha Colours

Most of the saris and dhotis produced in nineteenth- and early twentieth-century Bengal were woven in cream or white with accents of red, blue and black woven in the sari borders. So, kantha created in this period carries the same palette – the base cloth is cream and motifs are predominantly in blue, red and black, embroidered with coloured threads unravelled from the sari borders. However, this is not to say that other colours such as yellow and green were not used – they were just used less frequently. New coloured threads were also used to supplement recycled ones.

In contemporary times, men in urban areas of Bengal have largely transitioned away from wearing dhotis and lungis and have instead adopted Western-style clothing, as is the case in the majority of urban India. Meanwhile, urban Bengali women still cherish wearing saris, while including Western clothing styles in their wardrobes. However, traditional draped garments are still prevalent among men and women in rural areas and are fondly worn at festivals and ceremonies in Indian urban centres and diaspora gatherings across the world. Over time, kantha embroidery has also undergone changes, with the use of new, colourful base cloth replacing the once-ubiquitous recycled white cloth.

Despite being extraordinary documents of women's creativity, kantha textiles were often overlooked by curators, art historians and collectors due to their association with domesticity and women's labour. Kantha did not receive the same level of attention as other art forms such as paintings and sculpture from the region or even trade textiles. Sadly, because of the lack of interest in collecting or preserving them, no surviving examples of pre-nineteenth-century kantha are known to exist.

Further Afield

The tradition of quiltmaking using layers of discarded fabric embroidered with narrative iconography in running stitch also exists in the nearby state of Bihar, and is known as sujani. Quiltmaking processes, themes of rural life and nature, and motifs reflecting folklore bear striking similarities to the kantha of Bengal, suggesting cultural exchanges and assimilation of techniques.

▲ Sujani from Bihar in the collection of the National Crafts Museum, New Delhi.

Celebrating the Art of Kantha

When kantha began to be collected in the early 1900s by the Bengali intellectual elite – like civil servant Gurusaday Dutta, poet laureate Rabindranath Tagore, artist Abanindranath Tagore, and founder of the influential Bengal School of Art and artist Pratima Devi – for display at museums and exhibitions at eminent venues such as the Indian Society of Oriental Art and Art in Industry, Santiniketan, the focus was firmly on showcasing kantha as an assertion of a Bengali/Indian identity in the service of the anticolonial nationalist movement that swept the region at the time, as discussed by Pika Ghosh. The women who embroidered the kantha, however, received scant mention and their own descriptions of their work were not recorded.

When India rid herself of colonial rule and became independent in 1947, kantha were actively included in the collections of prestigious Indian museums, including the National Crafts Museum, the National Museum in Delhi, the Calico Museum of Textiles in Ahmedabad and Sanskriti Kendra, as well as in private collections.

According to Ghosh, the earlier convention of grouping embroidery under an anonymised 'handicraft' canon continued, despite many of the pieces carrying the stitched names of their makers. However, thanks to the efforts of a new generation of scholars, art historians, curators, artists, designers and makers, interest in kantha is growing globally and these undercelebrated testaments to women's creativity are finally beginning to receive their long-overdue credit.

◀ Gifts of love: Kantha embroidered with a (possible) dedication. Collection of the National Crafts Museum, New Delhi.

Kantha Taxonomy

Throughout my childhood, I spent countless hours at my mother's laboratory, exploring hundreds of chests of drawers that lined the walls; they were filled with insect specimens that were meticulously labelled with their scientific names. My mother was an entomological taxonomist – a scientist who specialised in identifying, naming and categorising insects. I was fascinated by the way she grouped insects into various species based on their morphological characteristics and other criteria. Drawing inspiration from my mother's work, I have used imagery and form to sort kantha into some broad categories.

▶ Kantha embroidered with a central *mandal* of lotus, trees of life, on the sides, and human and animal figures, embellished with paisleys and leaf borders. Collection of the National Crafts Museum, New Delhi.

Classification Based on Imagery

1. Illustrative Kantha

The highly illustrative style of kantha – commonly referred to as *nakshi* kantha – is characterised by its narrative-led approach and features scenic or figurative designs. *Nakshi* is derived from the Persian *naqsh*, which means 'design' or 'pattern'. This term became associated with illustrative kantha after Bengali poet Jasim Uddin's famous poem 'Nakshi Kanthar Math' ('The Field of the Embroidered Quilt') was published in 1928 – it is a tragic tale of two lovers, where the heroine embroiders her story on a kantha.

Nakshi kantha often show scenes from everyday life, folk art, deities, rituals and human figures embroidered alongside a vast array of flora- and fauna-inspired motifs. In the past, many of these works adhered to a classic layout, featuring a central *mandal* with a lotus flower, surrounded by concentric borders composed of floral, paisley and other patterns. Additional borders adorned the edges, while trees of life or paisleys decorated the corners, with various motifs interspersed throughout the ground.

Illustrative kantha feature an extensive stitch vocabulary, particularly in the pieces from the middle of the nineteenth century, where one can observe a diverse array of stitch techniques, such as running stitch, pattern darning, chain stitch, split stitch, satin stitch, cable stitch and many others. However, in more recent works, fewer stitch types tend to be used, with running stitch and darning stitch variations being the most prevalent.

Traditionally, women created highly personalised kantha. While some compositional conventions were followed, the designs were unique to each individual and evolved gradually over time, reflecting the artist's personal style

and preferences. However, with the increasing institutionalisation of kantha making, modern kantha produced for commercial purposes are often created with predetermined generic designs that are laid out on the fabric before stitching. As a result, the personal creative language that was once a hallmark of traditional kantha embroidery is now being replaced by more standardised designs.

▲ A square illustrative kantha (*bostani*) with the classic layout of a lotus blossom in the centre, paisleys in the corners and several rows of borders. Collection of the National Crafts Museum, New Delhi.

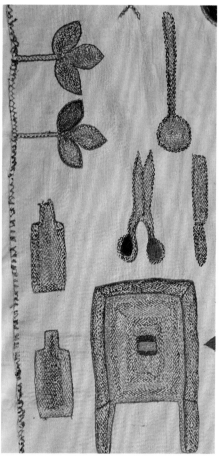

▲ Kantha motifs documenting rhythms and rituals of domestic life through everyday tools. Collection of the National Crafts Museum, New Delhi.

◄ Illustrative kantha embroidered with a plethora of motifs: domestic objects like ladles, a knife, a platter for serving *paan* (betel-leaf mouth freshener), animal figures (including an elephant, a horse and a peacock), human figures and a *rath* (a chariot carrying deities). Collection of the National Crafts Museum, New Delhi.

2. Abstract Geometric Kantha

This style of kantha is characterised by geometric motifs and tessellating patterns of shapes, such as squares, triangles, rhombuses and chevrons, arranged in grids, lattices or stripes. The geometric patterns may be used to represent objects encountered in daily life, but the representation is abstracted and stylised. Although there is an absence of figurative motifs, the patterns are rich in symbolism and often represent the maker's wishes for the intended recipient.

▶ (*Top*) Kantha embroidered with repeating circular motifs referencing *roti* or round flatbread.

▶ (*Bottom*) *Ruti* kantha with round motifs, symbolising roti, using a vibrant palette.

▼ Interesting use of fringes at the borders.

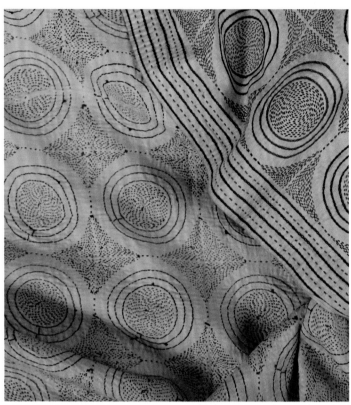

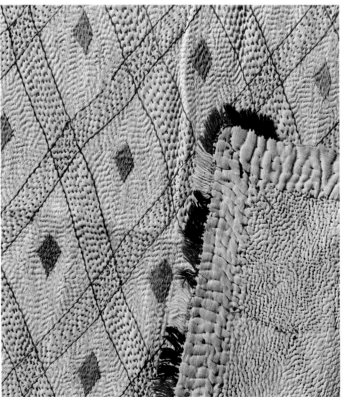

3. Botanical Kantha

This category of kantha is distinguished by the use of floral-inspired patterns, which may be arranged as an overall pattern or as directional designs. The designs often feature intricate depictions of flowers, leaves, vines and other foliage elements that are commonly found in the natural environment of the embroiderer.

The floral patterns in kantha embroidery are often symbolic and imbued with meaning, representing fertility, growth or simply the beauty of nature. They are a testament to the enduring connection between nature and artistic expression in traditional kantha embroidery.

▲ With its vibrant colours and abundance in Bengal, Joba flower (*Hibiscus rosa-sinensis*) is a popular motif in kantha embroidery of the Murshidabad region and is intricately embroidered in vivid red.

◀ (*Left*) Botanical forms in a variety of scales are used to embellish the kantha, along with a couple of birds. Collection of the National Crafts Museum, New Delhi.

◀ (*Right*) Vines featuring flowers, fish and birds form the central design, followed by a border of embroidered vines with leaves. Edges are adorned with a series of woven borders featuring swans and botanical motifs, probably salvaged from two different saris. Collection of the National Crafts Museum, New Delhi.

4. Geo-floral or Geo-figurative Designs

Kantha of this category often feature a combination of floral and geometric or figurative and geometric designs. Floral elements such as flowers, leaves, paisleys and other organic shapes are combined with geometric shapes and patterns like grids, lattices or stripes. The juxtaposition of these shapes results in visually dynamic compositions embodying deeply rooted symbolism. The style highlights the synergetic relationship between embroidery and weaving in Bengal, with jamdani patterns woven on the loom to emulate embroidery, and kantha borders embroidered to simulate woven sari borders.

In the example of this hybrid style (right), the embroiderer has incorporated stitched patterns emulating woven sari borders and the highly decorative embroidered paisleys in the corner, hinting at iconography drawn from the *jamawar* – woven Kashmir shawls. To me, all kantha styles – be they illustrative, abstract or hybrid – suggest the willingness of kantha embroiderers to be open to experimentation, and their ability to assimilate a wide variety of influences into their design language. It also suggests that women actively sought new forms of expression through stitch, evidencing the expansiveness of their creativity and their agency.

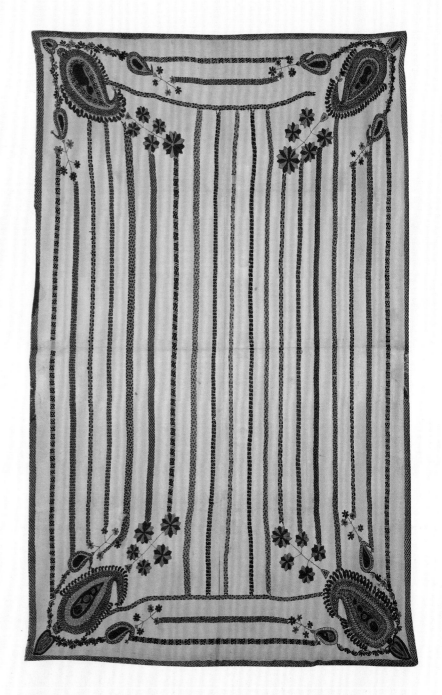

▶ (*Top*) Elaborately embroidered paisleys flank the corners of the kantha featuring stripes of border designs, referred to as *par tola* kantha. Collection of the National Crafts Museum, New Delhi.

▶ (*Left*) Geometric border designs emulating woven sari borders are embroidered in the body of this kantha, creating stripes. Collection of the National Crafts Museum, New Delhi.

▶ (*Right*) Detail of a geo-floral kantha featuring a grid embroidered with geometric patterns and flower wreathes on a quilted ground. Courtesy of Street Survivors India, Katna, Murshidabad.

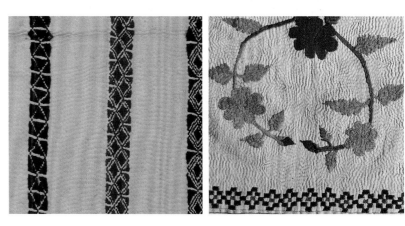

Classification Based on Form

Kantha are stitched in various sizes based on their intended use. This section discusses different forms of kantha.

1. Unembellished Utilitarian Kantha

Saris, dhotis and lungis softened by years of use and hundreds of washes are considered ideal for making kantha for swaddling infants or wrapping loved ones. A plain, functional kantha is created for everyday use by layering discarded saris and stitching them together with parallel rows of simple running stitches. These quilts are made in various sizes depending on their intended purpose. Large ones serve as bedspreads or light wraps for daily use, while smaller ones serve as pillowcases, mats, seats, swaddling cloth or baby quilts.

The tradition of making utilitarian quilts using cast-off clothing with simple stitches is prevalent throughout India. My grandmother frequently stitched quilts, reincarnating old saris, scraps and remnant fabrics into colourful spreads. Growing up in North India, I knew them as *gudris*. Patrick J. Finn notes the pan-India practice of quiltmaking using repurposed cloth in *Quilts of India*, 'Bengalis know them as kanthas; however the same quilt is termed *koudi* in Karnataka, *gudri* in Rajasthan and *dhakri* in Gujarat.'

▲ (*Top*) Utilitarian kantha drying in the courtyard, Murshidabad, West Bengal.

▲ (*Bottom*) Utilitarian kantha made with patches of patterned saris and chequered lungis, joined by simple running stitches.

37

2. Embellished Kantha

The embellished quilt developed into its own distinctive style in Bengal and is created in a range of sizes to suit a variety of intended purposes. Large bedspreads and rectangular wraps called *lep* kantha are made for warmth, while square pieces called *bostanis* or *baytons* are used for wrapping gifts, cherished valuables or books. Sujani kantha are highly decorative, thinner than *lep* kantha, and are made for special occasions or gifts. *Ashon* kantha are ornate seating mats for honoured guests or for use during weddings or *pooja* (Hindu worship), while *arshilata* are rectangular pieces for wrapping mirrors. *Oaar* kantha are pillow covers, while *durjani* are small purses created by folding in three corners of a square or rectangular kantha. *Gilaf* hold holy books and *chadar* kantha are used to cover tombs. *Bartan dhakni* or *rumal* are square pieces used as dish covers or to be gifted to a bridegroom as a handkerchief.

Women documented the rhythms of their domestic life and their personal perspectives on current events through stitching illustrative or abstract motifs on their kantha. This act of observing, reflecting, documenting and expressing personal experiences through kantha shows that the women were actively using their voice to register their presence and assert their views, rather than passively witnessing life. Creating kantha was a way of being fully present in their own lives and participating in the lives of their loved ones.

The kantha tradition continues to evolve into a multitude of forms to suit contemporary lifestyles in Bengal and beyond, from kantha wall art gracing gallery walls, to phone and laptop covers at work, dresses, saris and scarves in wardrobes, and bedspreads and cushions at home. As interest in kantha grows across the globe, it is important to remind ourselves of the essence of kantha making as an act of care towards using our planet's limited resources, an act of mindfulness to connect to our inner selves and to others, and an act of courage to express ourselves, regardless of external validation.

▼ *Arshilata* kantha is used to wrap a woman's toiletries and mirror. Collection of the National Crafts Museum, New Delhi.

▲ (*Above*) *Durjani* kantha coin purse, created by folding and stitching kantha corners. Collection of The Museum and Art Gallery, The Ramakrishna Mission Institute of Culture, Gol Park, Kolkata.

Stitch Techniques

Kantha has a rich vocabulary of stitches. While the running stitch and its variations are almost ubiquitously associated with kantha, there are several other stitch techniques that form part of its lexicon. These include back, split, chain, herringbone, satin, Holbein (and variations), buttonhole and detached chain stitches, as well as double darning and pattern darning variations. Several other stitch types are known to be used in kantha, including eye, zig-zag (and variations), seed, fern and cross stitches.

Anne Peranteau observes the use of more than forty-three different stitches in the Jill and Sheldon Bonovitz and the Stella Kramrisch Kantha Collections held at the Philadelphia Museum of Art, as documented by Darielle Mason in 2010. The richly diverse palette of stitches used by the kantha embroiderers shows not only the dexterity of their needles to express ideas in compelling ways but also their ability to assimilate a wide range of influences.

For ease of understanding, I will be discussing stitches under two broad categories: illustrative and abstract geometric kantha. However, it is important to note that several stitches cross over between both styles.

Knots for Starting & Finishing Off

In the vast majority of kantha examples that I studied, knots for starting and finishing off were clearly visible on the right-facing and reverse sides and at the edges. However, in some examples, especially on *dorukha* (a reversible kantha), knots were not visible. Instead, the stitch was begun with a small back stitch and finished off such that the end of the thread was cleverly embedded in the embroidery, without a visible knot. There is no rule as such for when to use a visible knot – it is an aesthetic decision, and one of many that the artist makes based on their own personal preference.

Quilter's Knot

Use a quilter's knot at the beginning to secure your thread to the fabric so the stitch doesn't come undone when you begin the embroidery.

If you are working on a reversible piece, use a small double stitch to begin, instead of the knot.

1 Thread your needle. Place the longer end of the thread over the index finger of your dominant hand, then hold your needle over it so that it forms an 'X'.

2 Wind the end of the thread two or three times around the needle.

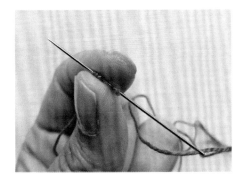

3 Hold the wound-up thread on the needle between the thumb and index finger of your non-dominant hand.

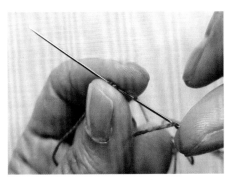

4 With the other hand, gently pull the needle through the wound-up thread, whilst still holding it between your finger and thumb.

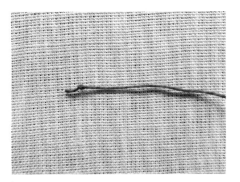

5 Pull the entire thread length through until only a small knot remains at the end. Snip off any excess thread with a pair of scissors, if needed.

41

Finishing Knot

You can make the finishing knots in
two ways:

*Method
one*

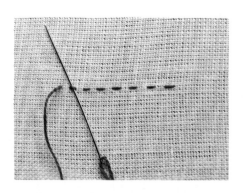

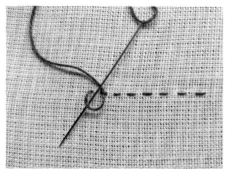

1 On the reverse side, insert the
needle under the nearest stitch,
without going through the fabric.

2 Pull through the stitch, leaving a
small length of thread below the
stitch line to form a loop. Pass the
needle under the loop.

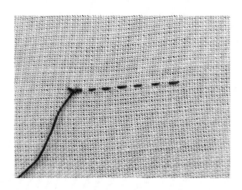

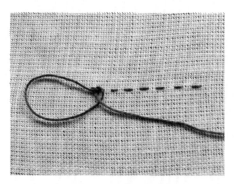

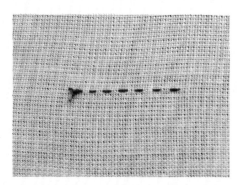

3 Pull through so that a small knot
forms at the end.

4 Repeat the steps again to make a
second knot, so it is robust.

5 Snip off extra thread length,
leaving a small tail of about half a
centimetre.

Method
two

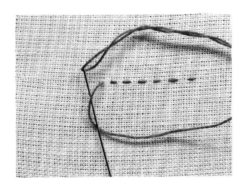

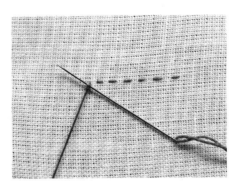

1 On the reverse side, make a loop with the thread. Bring the needle through the loop.

2 Pull through so a small knot is formed at the end. Use your needle, or finger, to help guide the knot down.

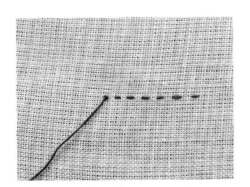

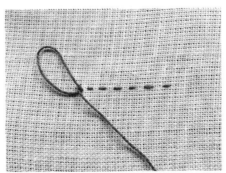

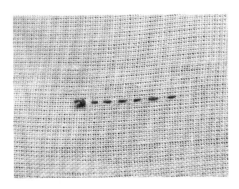

3 The small knot should sit right next to the surface of the fabric.

4 Repeat the previous steps to form a second knot. Take care that both knots sit atop one another and are not spread apart.

5 Snip off any extra thread length to tidy up.

Stitches in Illustrative Kantha

▶ A rich variety of stitches can be observed in this kantha quilt. Collection of the National Crafts Museum, New Delhi.

Outline Stitches

Stitches in this group are used to create linear elements like outlines of motifs, stems of flowers, and grids.

1. Running Stitch

Running stitch is the simplest and most fundamental of stitches used in numerous variations throughout the kantha lexicon. It has come to be considered synonymous with kantha and the terms are often used interchangeably. To create the running stitch, the needle is passed in and out of the fabric at regular intervals, resulting in a row of stitches that looks like a series of short lines with spaces between them.

As an artist, I am drawn to the simplicity and graphic quality of the running stitch. Its versatility in creating lines, motifs, patterns and texture makes the running stitch an exciting technique to work with. Just as a musician composes a symphony by adjusting the pitch, duration and arrangement of notes, one can create a diverse range of designs through playing with the characteristics of stitching, such as the length, spacing, thickness and direction.

The running stitch is used in kantha in slightly different ways. In utilitarian kantha, rows of running stitches are used to strengthen fragile layers for prolonged use. Stitches are often longer, coarser and worked in parallel lines from one end to the other, or in simple grids. However, in embellished kantha, it is employed for decorative purposes to create outlines of motifs and to fill in motifs, so the stitch size is smaller and finer.

Running stitches are also used to quilt layers together by working parallel rows of small stitches around the contours of motifs, which gather and sculpt the kantha surface into its characteristic rippled texture.

▲ Running stitch used as outline and filling stitch. Collection of the National Crafts Museum, New Delhi.

Just as a musician composes a symphony by adjusting the pitch, duration and arrangement of notes, one can create a diverse range of designs through playing with the characteristics of stitching, such as the length, spacing, thickness and direction.

Method

I find it easiest to move from right to left for running stitch, as I am right-handed. However, you may wish to try stitching from left to right or bottom to top. Stitch in any direction that feels comfortable to you.

Try changing the length of the stitches, the distance between each stitch or the gaps between stitched rows. Contrasts and variations make compositions more visually interesting and invite the viewer's eye to pause and linger.

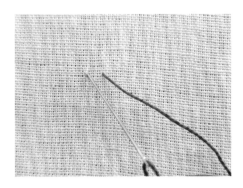

1 Begin with a knot or a back stitch to secure the thread.

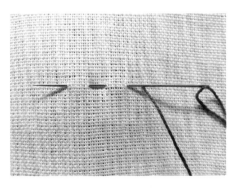

2 Bring your needle up through the fabric and make a few stitches at a time by passing the needle in and out of the fabric at equal distances.

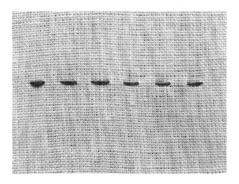

3 Finish off at the end of the row with a knot.

2. Darning Stitch

The darning stitch is similar to the running stitch. However, in darning stitches the stitch length is typically longer, rows are closer together and unlike the running stitch only a tiny length of fabric – often a single thread – is picked up from the base cloth with the needle between each darning stitch. The single thread gap results in giving darning stitch the appearance of couching, which is a decorative embroidery technique in which a thread is laid over the surface of the fabric and secured in place with a series of small stitches.

Darning stitch is a good option for mending holes or adding decorative details to embroidery projects. In kantha, the darning stitch is often used to outline motifs and figures. It is also used to create patterns, as discussed in more detail in the pattern darning section (see pages 66–76).

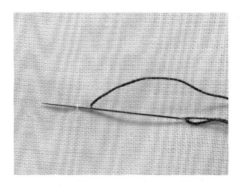

1 Bring your needle up to the surface and begin by taking a long float of stitch.

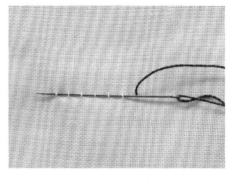

2 Pick up a small amount of fabric with your needle and make the next long float, leaving a small gap between the stitches.

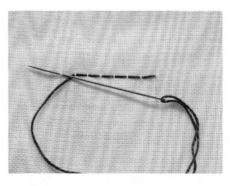

3 Continue taking long stitches in this way, pulling the thread taut as you go.

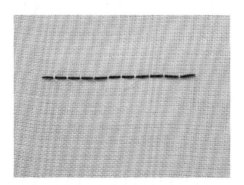

4 This will create a smooth, even line.

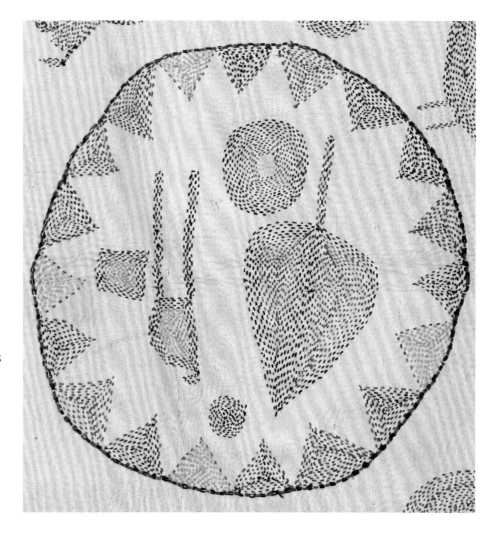

3. Double Darning/ Running Stitch

A versatile stitch, double darning/ running stitch is used for outlining motifs, creating sections and adding linear elements in kantha. The stitch is the same on both sides of the fabric. Repeated over an area, it can also be used to create texture.

▶ Here, double running stitch in red and black outlines the platter. Collection of the National Crafts Museum, New Delhi.

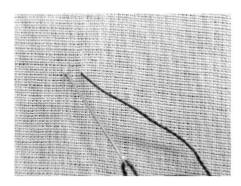
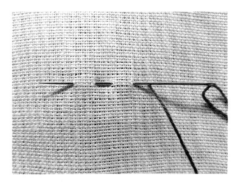
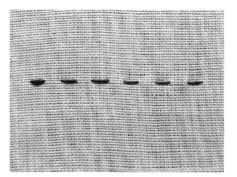

1 Make a row of evenly spaced running stitches, the stitch length being equal to the space between them.

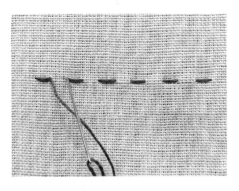

2 Using either the same-coloured thread or a contrast-coloured thread, fill in the gaps with an additional row of running stitches.

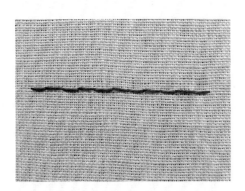

3 This will result in a continuous line of stitches, referred to as double running stitch. To create a solid filled-in area, repeat parallel rows of stitches placed closely such that no gap is visible between the rows.

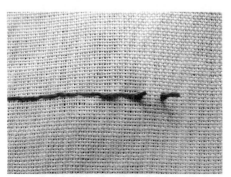

4 Finish off with a knot on the reverse. The stitch when used as filling is referred to as double darning stitch.

◀ Here, back stitch is used to outline the figures and illustrate facial features. Outfits are embellished with grid pattern darning. Embroidered by Pritikana Goswami, Hushnohana, Kolkata.

4. Back Stitch

Back stitch makes a continuous straight or curved line of stitches without any gaps in between.
In many areas of Bengal, this stitch is referred to as *bokhia*.

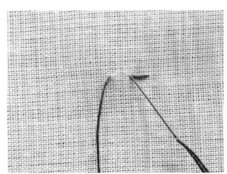

1 Make your first stitch, then bring your needle up to the top of the fabric a stitch length away.

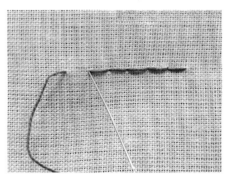

2 Make a stitch back, inserting your needle into the same hole where your previous stitch ended. Continue making stitches in this manner.

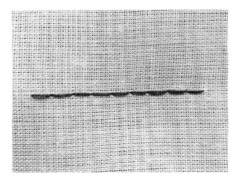

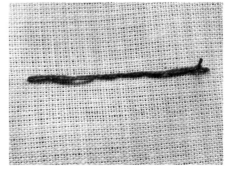

3 When the required length is done, finish off with a knot on the reverse.

5. Stem Stitch

Stem stitch, or *dal phor* in some Bengali areas, makes repeated stitches that seem to lie at an angle, giving a rope-like appearance. It has a raised texture and is easy to use for curved or straight lines, and so it lends itself to outlines of motifs, flower stems and text.

▶ The stem of the Tree of Life is embroidered with stem stitch. Collection of the National Crafts Museum, New Delhi.

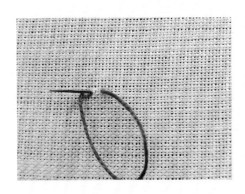

1 Bring your needle up at the start of the stitch line and insert it a short distance away.

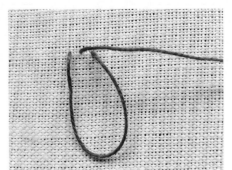

2 Pull the thread through the fabric, leaving the thread loose enough to make a small loop below the working line.

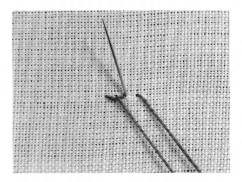

3 Next, bring your needle up halfway between the stitch length and pull through so the slack of the loop is tightened.

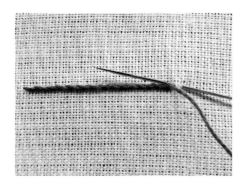 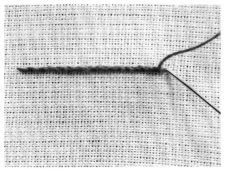 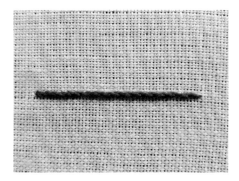

4 Make another looped stitch, equal in length to the first. Bring your needle up at the end of the previous stitch and repeat to continue.

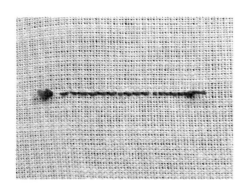

5 When the required length is done, finish off with a knot on the reverse.

6. Chain Stitch

Chain stitch is formed by a series of interconnected loops, with each loop secured by the subsequent one. This stitch is commonly used in kantha as both an outline and a filling stitch.

It is worth noting that, historically, the chain stitch has had a significant role in the region. The sought-after Satgaon quilts or Colcha quilts, commissioned by the Portuguese and English in the sixteenth and seventeenth centuries from the Satgaon region of Bengal, employed the chain stitch to create highly intricate designs, typically depicting a combination of classical, biblical and Hindu themes in monochrome tussar silk thread on cotton ground. The stitch is also employed in kantha with great dexterity.

▶ Chain stitches form the stem of the flower and embellish the border band, and buttonhole stitch is used at edges of the piece. Collection of the National Crafts Museum, New Delhi.

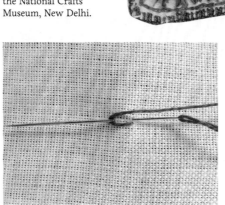

1 Bring your needle up to the surface of the fabric. Insert the needle again, close to where you came up first, placing the thread underneath the needle to form a loop, and pull through.

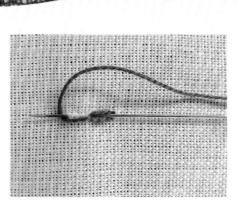

2 Insert needle at the tip of the loop.

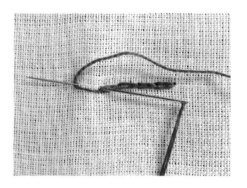
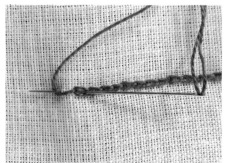
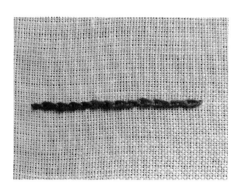

3 Continue stitching, forming a linked row or a chain of stitches.

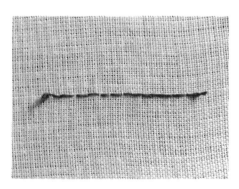

4 When the required length is done, finish off with a knot on the reverse.

Colcha quilts from the Satgaon region of Bengal, employed the chain stitch to create highly intricate designs, typically depicting a combination of classical, biblical and Hindu themes.

7. Cable Stitch

A variation of the chain stitch, the cable stitch is created by alternating straight stitches and loops to achieve an appearance similar to a metal chain. It is often used to embroider straight or curved lines, for instance stems in floral designs.

Method one

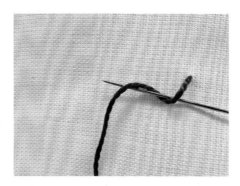

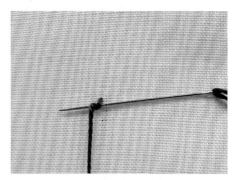

1 Bring the needle and thread to the right-facing side. Wrap the thread once around the needle, keeping the needle close to the surface.

◄ Pattern darning stitches have been used in this Tree of Life for filling the leaf shape and cable stitch has been used for the stem. Collection of the National Crafts Museum, New Delhi.

Method two

If you prefer not to do the wrapping and making the chain in one step, you can break the steps down further:

1 Bring the needle to surface Wrap the thread once around the needle.

2 Insert the needle a short distance away. Pull through while leaving a small loop on the surface.

3 Bring your needle through this loop to make a loop of the chain

4 Repeat to continue.

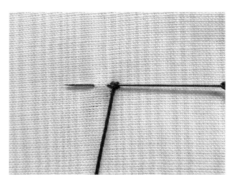

2 Insert the needle into the fabric a few millimetres ahead and bring the tip of the needle out a stitch distance away.

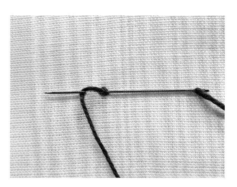

3 Take the thread behind the needle to complete the chain, and pull through.

4 Wrap the thread around the needle again and repeat to continue.

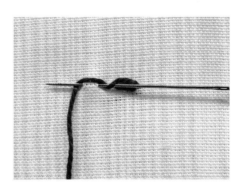

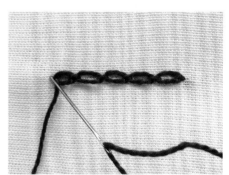

8. Split Stitch

This technique is similar to back stitch, except that the needle splits the centre of the preceding stitch instead of emerging from the same hole, resulting in a stitch that resembles a small chain stitch. There are two ways to make split stitch.

Method one

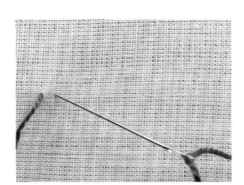

1 Bring your needle and thread up to the right-facing side and insert the needle back into the fabric a stitch length away, forming a straight stitch.

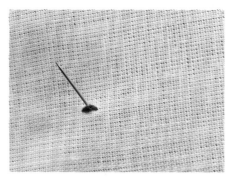

2 Bring the needle up at the centre of the stitch, splitting the thread, and pull through.

3 Make the second stitch by inserting the needle forward, ensuring that the length is equal to the first stitch.

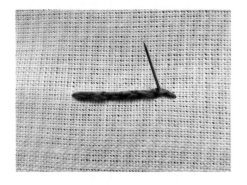

4 Continue along the design line by repeating the steps.

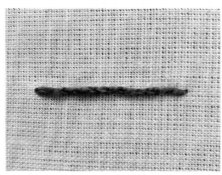

5 When the required length is done, finish off with a knot on the reverse.

◀ This detail shows the use of split stitch and chain stitch. Collection of the National Crafts Museum, New Delhi.

Method two

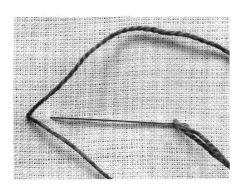

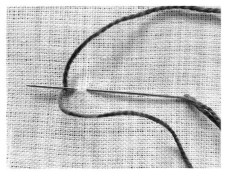

1 Bring your threaded needle up and separate the strands in two with your hands. Alternatively, work with doubled-up perle thread and separate the two strands.

2 Insert your needle into the fabric a stitch distance away. Emerge halfway across that stitch length and pull though.

3 Repeat to continue.

4 Finish with a small anchoring stitch at the end of the line, on the reverse.

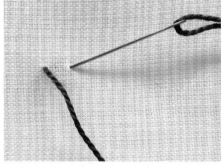

9. Fly Stitch

Fly stitch is used in borders or the body of the kantha. When repeated multiple times, it forms a line.

▲ A series of fly stitches have been used in the borders. Collection of the National Crafts Museum, New Delhi.

1 Imagine or draw a vertical line. Bring your needle up to the left of that line, and insert it horizontally across to the right of the line.

2 Find a point diagonally below between your two stitches, and bring the needle out over your working thread.

3 Pull through so that the stitch forms the letter 'V'. Anchor it with a small straight stitch at the base of the V, forming the fly stitch.

4 Repeat, leaving a short gap between each fly stitch.

▶ Traditional pattern in kantha: a floral shrub with delicate undulating branches placed in an urn. Courtesy of Street Survivors India, Katna, Murshidabad.

◀ (*Overleaf*) Kantha with floral vines embroidered with *mala phor* in the stems. Courtesy of Street Survivors India, Katna, Murshidabad.

10. Mala Stitch or Double Chain Stitch Variation

I was unfamiliar with *mala* stitch, before my research trip to Murshidabad (see page 84), since I had not come across it in publications or kantha examples. In Katna, this stitch is referred to by several names, including *geent phansh*, *mala phor* or *bichhe phor*, and is often used for embroidering long, straight or curved lines such as stems and trellises in floral kantha. *Geent* means a knot in Bengali, while *mala* means a garland or a necklace made of flowers or beads.

Traditional floral patterns include *ek jhari* kantha, which features an urn or vase motif from which a single floral vine or *jhari* radiates outward in a symmetrical pattern. Another example is *char khari* kantha or *aatu jhari* kantha, which features patterns with four or eight branches. It is worth noting that regional names of stitches and patterns can vary.

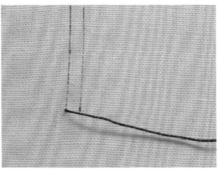

1 Draw two parallel lines as guides to aid your stitch placement. (With practice, you can do away with drawing the lines and imagine them by following the grain of the fabric.) You can work from bottom to top, positioning your lines vertically, or right to left horizontally. I find it easier to work from bottom to top. Bring your needle up at the bottom of your left line.

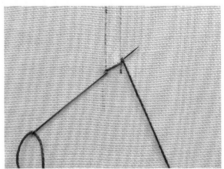

2 Insert the needle in the same hole that you came up from and emerge slightly higher, diagonally across on the right line. Loop your thread under the needle from the left of the needle to the right. Cross the thread over the needle so the working thread is to the right of the needle and pull through.

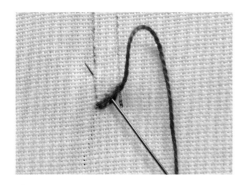

3 Insert your needle near the base of the stitch, just below the crossover, and emerge on the left line.

4 Form a stitch here by looping the thread under the needle from left to right and pull through.

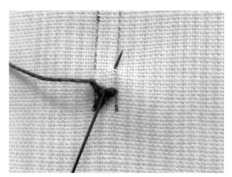

5 Next, insert your needle in the small triangular shape in the loop and emerge on the right line.

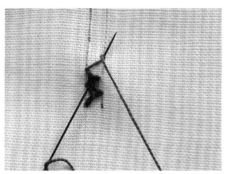

6 Continue by alternating stitches on the left and right lines.

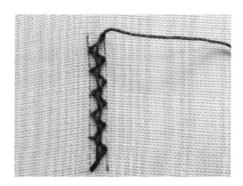

7 When finishing the stitch, take your needle down over the last loop to form a small anchoring stitch.

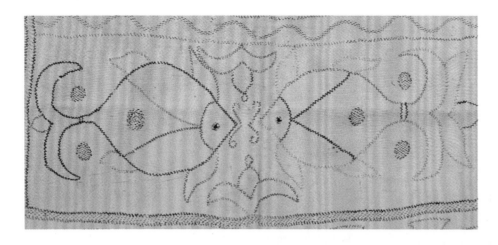

◁ Herringbone stitch
is used to illustrate the
outlines of two large
fish, borders and floral
motifs. Collection of
the National Crafts
Museum, New Delhi.

11. Herringbone Stitch

The versatility of herringbone
stitch makes it a popular choice
in illustrative as well as abstract
geometric kantha.

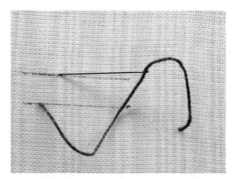

1 Draw or imagine two parallel lines.
Bring your needle up at the start of
the first line and take it across to the
parallel line, making a diagonal stitch.

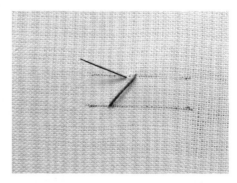

2 Bring your needle back up a short
distance across from where it
went down.

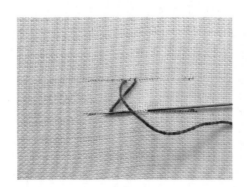

3 Take the needle diagonally across
to the opposite line.

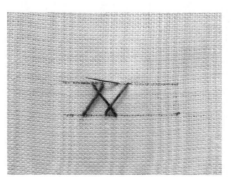

4 Bring your needle up on the same
line, taking a small pinch of the
fabric, and pull through.

5 Take your needle diagonally across
to form your next stitch. Continue
until the desired length is filled.

◀ A series of cross stitches have been used to form the stem of this plant. Collection of the National Crafts Museum, New Delhi.

12. Cross Stitch

Cross stitches embroidered in a series are used for making outlines, creating grids and filling motifs. *Galicha* (carpet) kantha are embroidered with cross stitches in vibrant geometric patterns that often cover the entire surface of the kantha.

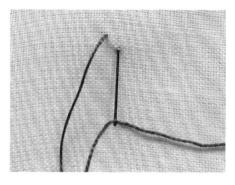

1 Bring your needle up and take it diagonally down to form a diagonal straight stitch.

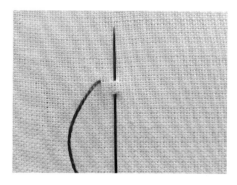

2 Bring the needle up again, straight above where you went in, aligning it to the beginning of the first stitch.

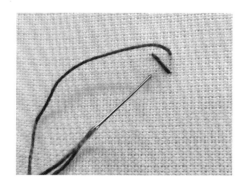

3 Pull through and insert the needle in the opposite corner to form your first cross.

4 Repeat to continue.

65

Filling Stitches

This group includes stitches that are used to fill motifs and shapes, create borders and fill the ground or field of kantha.

1. Pattern Darning

As explored by Virginia Colton, pattern darning uses parallel rows of straight stitches of different lengths to create a design. Stitch rows are placed side by side with no gaps visible between consecutive rows. The appearance of stitched areas resembles satin stitch, with the important distinction that satin stitch is identical on both sides, while pattern darning only appears on the front of the fabric.

Pattern darning is highly versatile and frequently used in kantha to fill both organic and geometric motifs, and to create geometric patterns in the borders. The warp and weft threads are counted, and the stitch length and spaces between stitches are gradually increased or decreased with each successive row, so that the pattern is precise.

Changing the distance between stitches or the gap between stitched rows offers scope for variation, resulting in a plethora of patterns, each known by a specific name. Stitched patterns in kantha borders emulate woven sari border patterns.

◀ Motifs embroidered with chevron, filling and diagonal pattern darning by Mahua Lahiri, Hushnohana, Kolkata. The piece takes inspiration from the Manoda Sundori Kantha in the Gurusaday Museum.

▶ Detail showing use of pattern darning as a line and filling stitch. Collection of the National Crafts Museum, New Delhi.

Pattern darning is highly versatile and frequently used in kantha to fill both organic and geometric motifs, and to create geometric patterns in the borders.

2. Filling Pattern Darning

Called *bhorat phor* in Bengali, meaning 'to fill', this stitch is used for filling motifs. Rows of long, straight stitches are made, separated by the smallest of gaps just catching the fabric, usually only as wide as a single thread. A long stitch is made, picking up one thread from the base fabric before making the next long stitch. By making several rows in this way, this darning stitch can fill motifs with patterns.

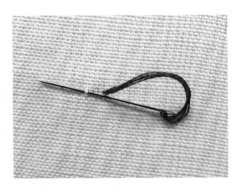

1 Bring your needle up and insert it into the fabric a short distance away. Next, pick up a single warp or weft thread with the tip of your needle.

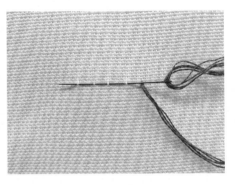

2 Place as many stitches on your needle as you comfortably can.

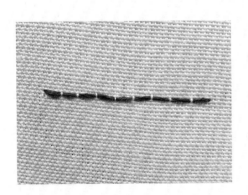

3 Pull the thread through. The key is to be consistent in the stitch length and the gap between the stitches. Continue working to the edge of your motif.

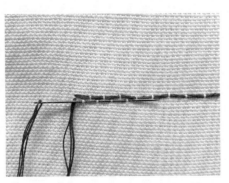

4 To begin the next row, bring up your needle such that no gap is visible between the rows.

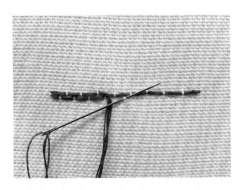

5 Continue to stitch, keeping the placement of the single thread gap either in exactly the same position as the preceding row or alternating the placement, as in a brick wall.

▲ Kamadhenu (divine bovine goddess), Shiva's figure and Parvati's bodice have been embroidered with filling pattern darning stitch (*koshida*). Embroidered by members of Hushnohana, Kolkata.

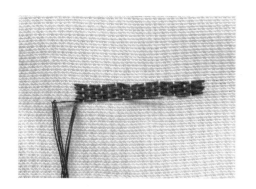

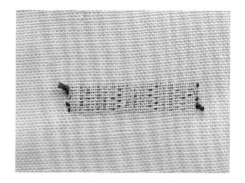

6 As the stitch is done on the top layer of the quilt only, without going through the other layers, the stitches do not appear on the reverse.

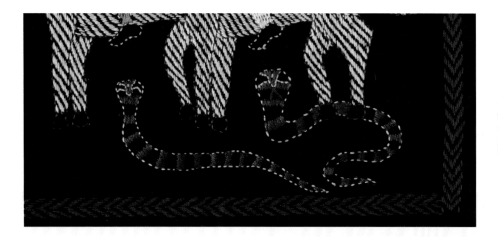

◀ Serpents have been embroidered
with stripe pattern darning,
and the borders in chevron
pattern darning by members
of Hushnohana, Kolkata.

3. Stripe Pattern Darning

In this variation of the darning stitch,
a row of stitches is made with a longer
gap between them, followed by
several rows of stitches placed next to
the preceding one, without any gaps
visible, to achieve the appearance
of stripes. The distance between
individual stitches may vary as per the
preference of the embroiderer and
the shape of motif to be filled.

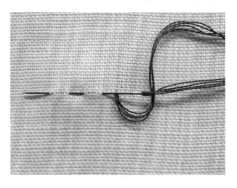

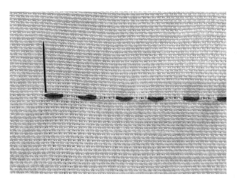

1 Make a row of stitches and leave a
large enough space between each
to suit your motif or pattern.

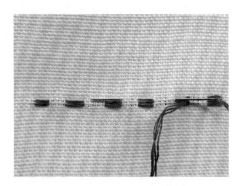

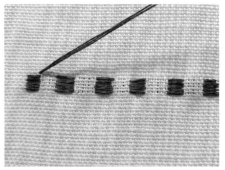

2 Align successive rows in exactly
the same position so that the
stitches and blank spaces between
the stitches align with those of the
preceding and succeeding rows.

▶ Variations of pattern darning can be seen in this kantha including chevron, spiral and diagonal stripe styles.

▶ Fish motifs have been embroidered with chevron pattern darning.

4. Chevron Pattern Darning

Often referred to as *dhaner shish* (ear of the paddy) or *maach kaata* (fish bone) in Bengali, this stitch is used to create bands in kantha borders and to fill motifs.

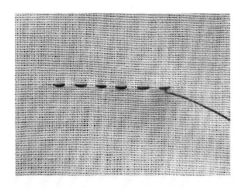

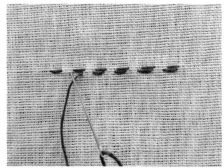

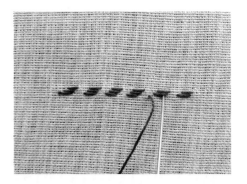

1 Begin with stitching a single row of running stitches, keeping the gaps between stitches an equal length to the stitch.

2 Turn your fabric around to make the next row of stitches. To begin the second row, insert your needle adjacent to the midpoint of the first stitch. Follow the grain and bring the needle up halfway across the gap. Continue scooping up sections of fabric to make several stitches at once, ensuring the length of stitches and gaps is the same as the first row. Pull through.

3 Turn the fabric around to make the third row. Begin by inserting the needle in the middle of the first stitch in the second row and emerge halfway across the gap between the stitches of the preceding row, still following the grain.

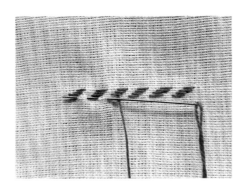

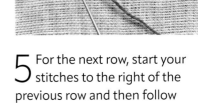

4 Make four to five rows in a similar manner.

5 For the next row, start your stitches to the right of the previous row and then follow steps 2–4.

6 Alternate the direction to create a zig-zag pattern. Ensure that the size of the stitches and gaps is identical on both sides.

▶ This example illustrates bending stitch spiral motif in circular pattern darning. Collection of the National Crafts Museum, New Delhi.

5a. Circular Pattern Darning: Spiral Motif

Two types of motifs are created in this very popular form of darning in kantha: the spiral and the wheel. The spiral motif, also known as *shostir chinho* or *chalta phool* (the moving flower), is a form of pattern darning that involves the placement of stitches in concentric circles with each stitch moving slightly forward in successive rows.

The stitch length varies with each successive row, depending on whether the embroidery is started from the centre and worked towards the periphery or started from the periphery and worked towards the centre. When the stitch is initiated from the centre, the stitch length progressively increases with each subsequent row, whereas if started from the periphery, the stitch length progressively decreases with each successive row.

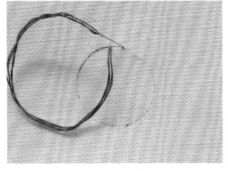

1 Draw a circle on your fabric with an erasable pen. Decide on the length of your stitch and make running stitches along the periphery of the circle.

2 To begin the second row of stitches, bring your needle up next to any stitch on the first circle, so that your needle is placed slightly ahead of the base of the stitch in the previous row. Insert the needle back into the fabric, slightly ahead of the stitch in the previous row. Complete the circle.

3 Continue working in concentric circles, decreasing the stitch length with each successive round until you reach the centre of the circle.

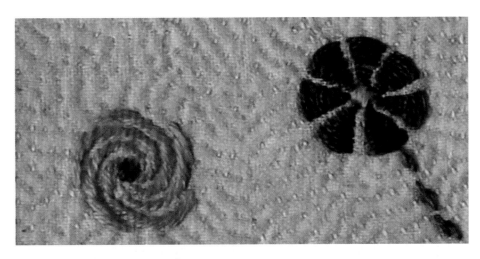

▷ The spiral (left) and wheel (right) have been embroidered using circular pattern darning. Embroidered by Hushnohana, Kolkata.

5b. Circular Pattern Darning: Wheel Motif

The wheel motif can be worked from the centre outwards, or inwards. In Kolkata, West Bengal, this motif is referred to as *ucchay phool* or *chakra* (the wheel) – names in other regions can vary.

Stitches are placed in concentric rows, decreasing in length with each successive row if the motif is worked inwards towards the centre from the periphery, or increasing in length if worked from the centre outwards. I find it easier to stitch from the periphery towards the centre.

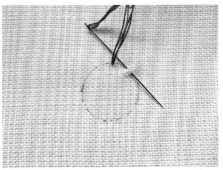

1 Draw a circle on your fabric with an erasable pen. Decide on the length of your stitch and make running stitches along the periphery of the circle, keeping the gap between the stitches small.

2 Decrease the stitch length with each successive row. To begin the second row of stitches, bring your needle up next to any stitch on the first circle, so that no space will be visible between the stitched rows.

3 Insert the needle back into the fabric, taking a stitch. The length of your stitch should be slightly shorter than the stitch in the preceding row. Continue until you have gone around the circle.

4 Continue working in concentric circles, decreasing the stitch length from each end with each successive circle, until you reach the centre of the circle.

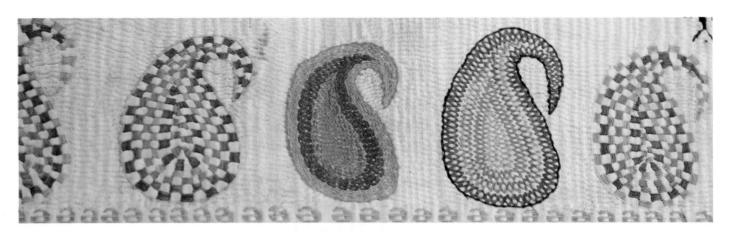

▼ Paisley embroidered with grid pattern darning. Collection of the National Crafts Museum, New Delhi.

6. Grid Pattern Darning

Grid pattern darning is a technique that involves stitching alternating bands of pattern darning to create chequered grids. This technique is used to fill motifs in the field of kantha and also to create borders. Stitching is done in contrasting-coloured threads, as in the paisleys above or in a single colour to create a repeating chequered pattern. Both options are equally popular.

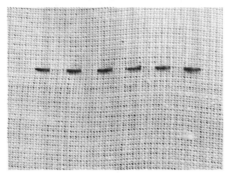

1 Create a row of running stitches that are equal in length to the gaps between the stitches.

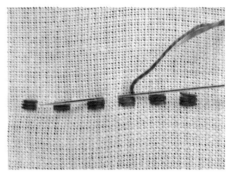

2 Stitch several identical rows, ensuring the stitches and gaps follow the same placement as the previous rows.

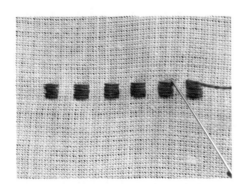

3 Continue stitching until the rows of stitches appear as a series of squares.

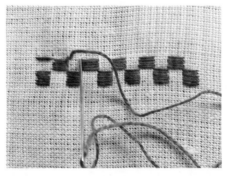

4 For the next section, change the placement of the stitches so they correspond to the gaps (and the gaps correspond to the stitches) in the previous section.

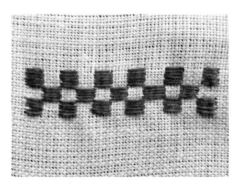

5 Continue in this way until a grid is formed.

7. Bending Stitch or Diagonal Bands Pattern

Niaz Zaman refers to this as the bending stitch or *kaitya* (ant line). A variation of running stitch, this pattern is created by working close rows of running stitches parallel to each other and moving each stitch slightly forward in successive rows. The embroidered rows give the appearance of diagonal bands of stitches. Several patterns used in borders are derived from variations of this stitch, and each has its own regional name.

1 Make a row of running stitches. Keep the stitch length equal to the gap between stitches.

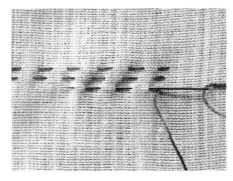

2 Move the stitch slightly forward in the second row, ensuring the length of stitch and gap remains the same as in the first row.

3 Continue making successive rows, moving your stitch slightly forward in each row.

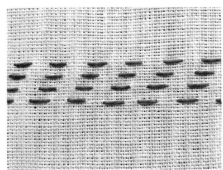

4 Now follow the same method, moving the stitch slightly back with each row to create the pattern.

8. Convent Stitch/ Bokhara Couching

This is a self-couching technique as it uses a single thread instead of the two sets of threads used in classic couching. It is often used to fill in large motifs on kantha. In Murshidabad, embroiderers refer to this stitch as *silai phor*, while in Kolkata this stitch is known as *koshida* or *Kashmiri bhorat* (Kashmiri filling stitch). The name is perhaps a nod to the embroidery used in Kashmiri shawls.

The stitch is worked in two steps: a long stitch is taken and then another smaller stitch is taken across it to hold it in place. If your stitch is longer than 1.5cm (⅝in), I suggest making two or more anchoring stitches so that the long stitch retains its shape. In kantha, two versions of this stitch are known to be used: convent stitch and Bokhara couching.

Convent Stitch Method

In convent stitch, small anchoring stitches are taken to couch the long laid threads. The needle comes from the right of the stitched line to the left to form anchoring stitches. The placement of anchoring stitches is spread out across the design in a random fashion.

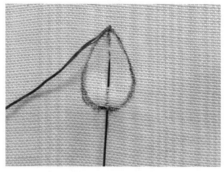

1 Draw your motif shape, such as a leaf, with a vertical line in the centre. Make a long stitch from the tip to the base of the shape, bringing your needle out partway along the central line, emerging to the right of the long stitch.

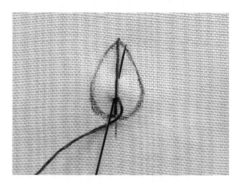

2 Make a small anchoring stitch by crossing over to the left side of the long stitch, and bringing your needle back out diagonally a short distance above on the right half.

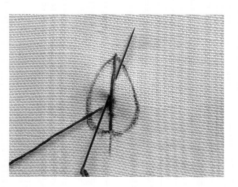

3 Repeat step 2 and make another short anchoring stitch.

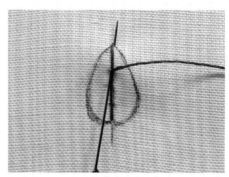

4 Bring your needle up on the periphery of the motif, adjacent to the first stitch.

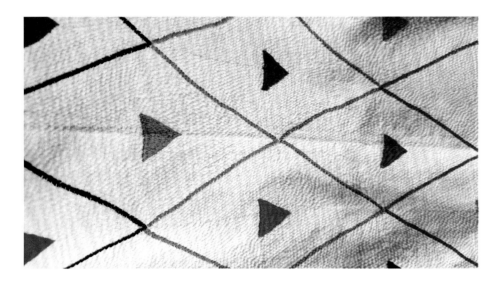

◄ Colourful triangles stitched with Bokhara couching/Kashmiri stitch placed inside a diamond-shaped grid, embroidered with herringbone stitches in abstract geometric kantha. Courtesy of Street Survivors India, Katna, Murshidabad.

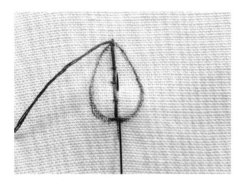

5 Make a second long stitch by bringing the needle down to the base of the motif, coming out above the anchoring stitch you made in step 2, and continue until you reach the tip.

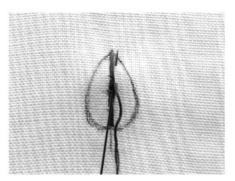

6 Repeat the smaller stitches to hold this stitch down by spacing them out, so they are not aligned but instead are scattered around. As a variation, you may also wish to align them, so the anchoring stitch appears in a row.

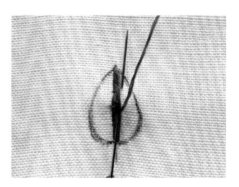

7 Continue making a long stitch, and then anchoring stitches, until you reach the right-hand edge of your motif.

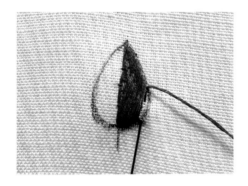

8 On both halves of your shape, remember to bring your needle up on the right side of the long stitch and insert it across to the left to make a small anchoring stitch.

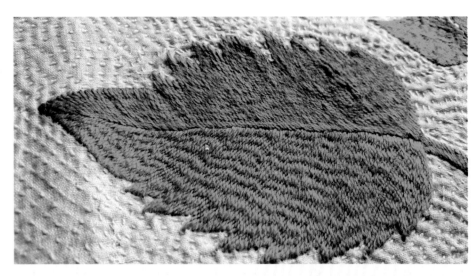

▶ Bokhara couching is shown on this leaf design. Courtesy of Street Survivors India, Katna, Murshidabad.

Bokhara Couching Method

The Bokhara couching method involves taking slightly longer diagonal stitches to anchor the long laid threads. The couching stitches are placed in specific positions to form a secondary pattern on top of the laid threads. It is a self-couching technique so you work with only one set of threads instead of the two used in conventional couching.

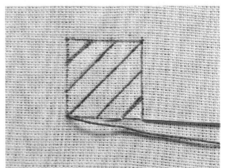

1 Draw your motif, such as a square, and add diagonal guidelines where you'd like the couching to be visible. Begin with a long, straight stitch from the left-hand side of the motif to the right. You can also work top to bottom. Emerge on the couching line, above the straight stitch.

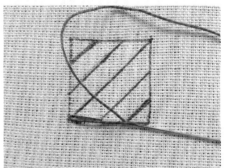

2 Make a small diagonal stitch over the long straight stitch (to secure it) and emerge on the second couching line marked on the cloth.

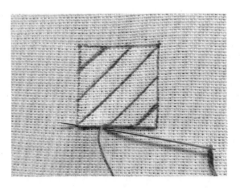

3 Make another diagonal stitch and bring your needle up at the edge of the motif to complete the line.

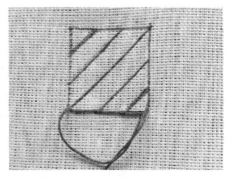

4 Make another long, straight stitch from left of the motif to the right. Repeat steps 1–4 to couch.

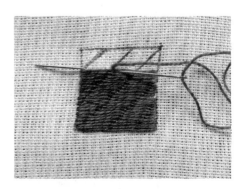

5 Continue couching in this way until your motif is fully filled in.

9. Fishbone Stitch

Fishbone stitch, also called *khejur chhori*, is used for creating and filling motifs.

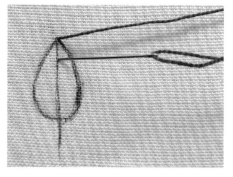

1 Bring your needle up at the top of your motif, such as the tip of a leaf. Make a small vertical stitch on the spine.

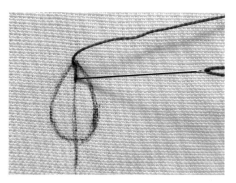

2 Come out from the left of the vertical stitch and cross over, without leaving a gap, to insert the needle to the right of the central stitch.

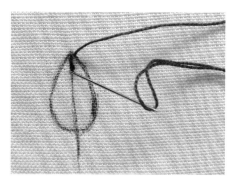

3 Come out by the top right of the central stitch and go back in at the bottom left of the central line.

4 Continue alternating your stitches until the motif is filled.

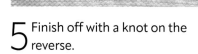

5 Finish off with a knot on the reverse.

10. Jali Stitch

Jali means 'a mesh' in Bengali. This stitch is similar in appearance to cross stitch. It is used to fill motifs and create textured areas in the kantha.

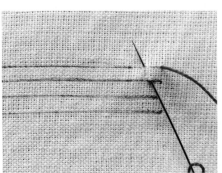 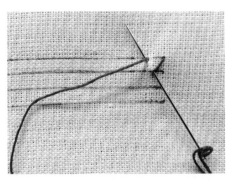

1 Draw four horizontal lines with a 5mm (¼in) gap between each. Starting at one end of the top line, come down to the lower line at a diagonal angle, and then bring your needle back out on the top line, to the left of where you began, to make a short diagonal stitch.

2 Bring your needle up, going up diagonally onto the lower line. Make a diagonal stitch by inserting your needle in the same hole where your first stitch ended (letter 'V').

◄ Here the birds and fish are stitched using *jali* stitch. Collection of the National Crafts Museum, New Delhi.

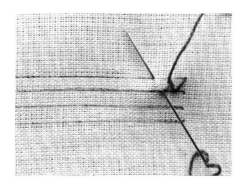

3 Come up at the top of the 'V', passing your needle through the same hole.

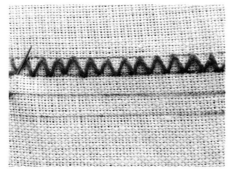

4 Repeat until you have made a line of 'V' stitches.

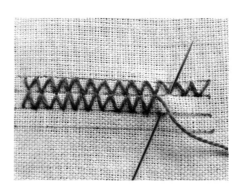

5 Continue on the following line underneath the first line of stitches.

6 Repeat to make a third row.

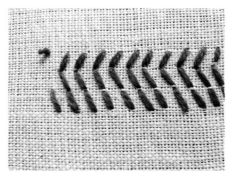

7 Finish off with a knot on the reverse.

Jali stitch is used to fill motifs and create textured areas in the kantha.

Stitches in Abstract Geometric Kantha

My research took me to Katna village in the Murshidabad district of West Bengal where my gracious host, Shabnam Ramaswamy, introduced me to the distinctive abstract and floral kantha of the region. Shabnam, with her late husband Jugnu, established the NGO Street Survivors of India which focuses on education and social justice and women's empowerment, and now employs over 1,500 women in the rural region.

Geometric shapes, including triangles, rhombuses, squares and rectangles, tessellate to create patterns. In the Murshidabad region, four primary categories of stitches are used to create abstract geometric kantha patterns:

1   Running stitch and pattern darning combination

2   Running stitch and detached chain stitch combination

3   Holbein stitch and variations

4   Interlaced stitches

It is worth noting that these stitches can be used on their own as well as in combination with other filling stitches like pattern darning (see pages 66–76) and convent stitch (see pages 78–81).

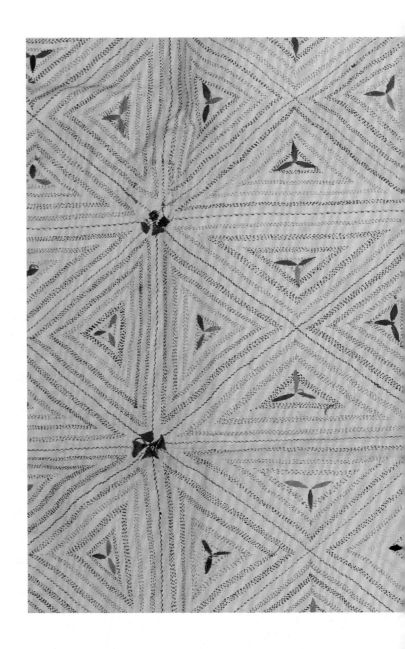

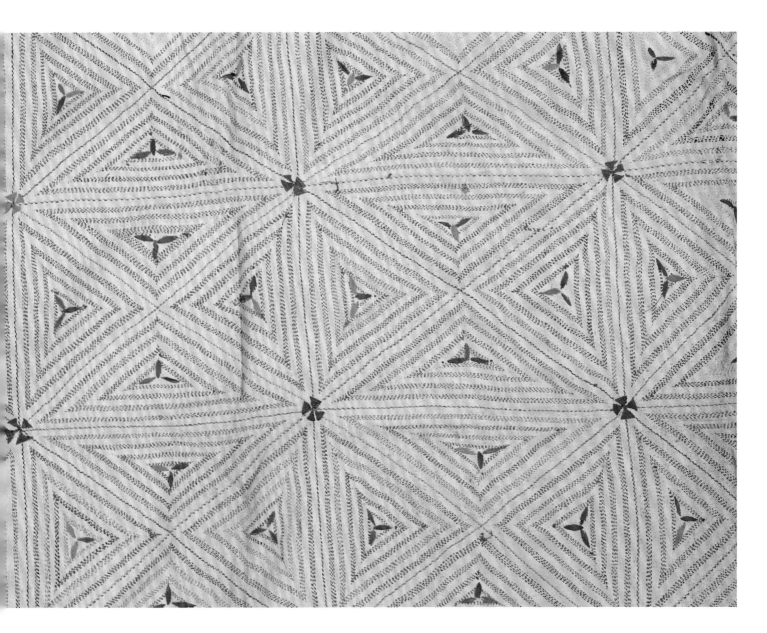

1. Kantha With Running Stitch and Pattern Darning Combination

▶ Abstract geometric kantha with diamond pattern in the body, embroidered with interlaced running stitch and diamonds filled in with *koshida bhorat*. Collection of the Street Survivors India, Katna, Murshidabad.

2. Kantha With Running Stitch and Detached Chain Stitch Combinations

Kantha embroidered with geo-abstract designs using running stitch and detached chain stitch (or lazy daisy stitch) are known as *phansher* kantha (*phansh* means 'a loop') in Murshidabad. As the name suggests, lazy daisy stitch loops are employed to create patterns, alongside parallel rows of running stitches by carefully placing the loops and running stitches in intricately designed patterns. These kantha are rich in symbolism and feature a dazzling variety of highly abstract geometric patterns that represent a range of objects encountered in daily life.

This method will take you through the steps of creating a pattern with five rows of stitches. However, you can reduce or increase the number of rows to make other patterns; the process will remain the same.

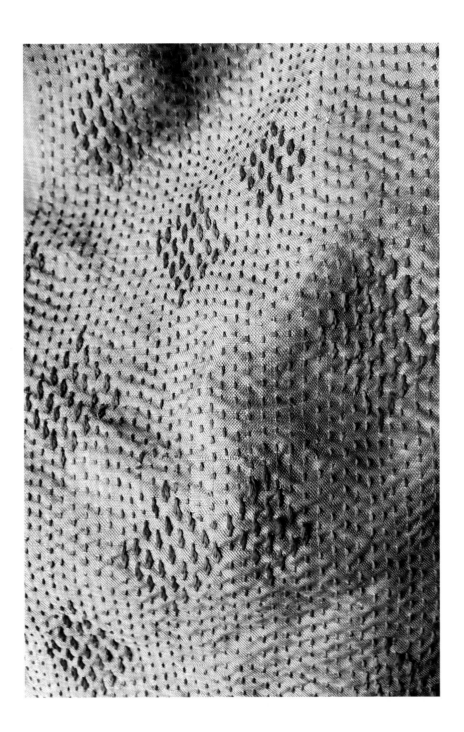

▷ Abstract geometric kantha made with a combination of running stitch and detached chain stitch. Courtesy of Street Survivors India, Katna, Murshidabad.

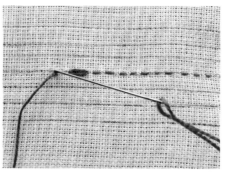

◀ Geometric embroidery patterns on kantha often emulate those on woven mats used as floor coverings. Both of these were made by members of Street Survivors India, Katna, Murshidabad.

1 Draw five horizontal lines with a 5mm (¼in) gap between the rows. Make a row of running stitches in the middle line up to the halfway point and then bring your needle up at the centre of the line. Make a detached chain stitch by taking your needle down in the same hole and come up a stitch distance away. Take the thread under the needle to form a loop and pull through. Make a small stitch to anchor the chain.

2 To make the next detached chain stitch, come up with your needle and thread a short gap away, insert the needle down in the same hole and bring it up a stitch length away. Take the thread under the needle, pull through and make a short anchoring stitch.

3 Make four (or as many you wish) detached chain stitch loops in this way.

4 Continue making several small running stitches to space the pattern. End the line by taking the needle down to the reverse and coming up at the row above.

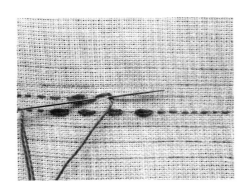 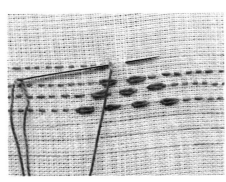 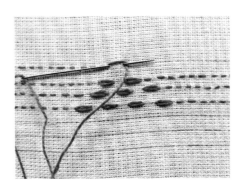

5 On the row above, continue with running stitch then make three detached chain stitch loops, placing them in alternating spaces with the stitches in the previous row.

6 Reduce the number of detached chain stitches and increase the number of running stitches in each successive row until you have a single chain stitch on the top row, with running stitches either side of it.

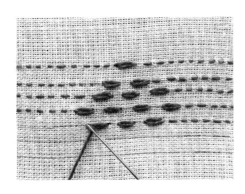 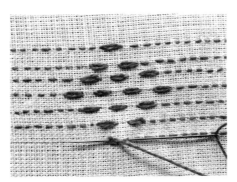 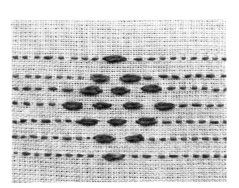

7 Repeat, working below the middle line and again decreasing the detached chain stitches by one each time.

8 You should now have a diamond pattern of chain stitches, surrounded by running stitch lines.

Motifs and Patterns Using Running Stitch and Detached Chain Stitch Combinations

The following patterns are made by combining running stitches and detached chain stitches:

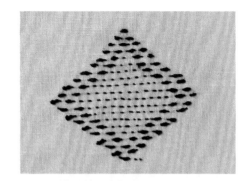

▲ Aaina Khopa (mirror).

▲ Toffee.

▲ Tara Chutki (little stars).

▲ Lathi (stick).

▲ Aaina Khopa Manjhe Machi (mirror bun with fly).

▲ Haath Dharo Dhari Mudha (stools holding hands).

▲ Paan Phaansh (paan is an after-dinner treat – refreshing ingredients are wrapped in a betel leaf).

▲ Angoor Thoopa (grapes).

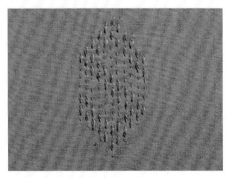

▲ Angrezi 'S' (the English letter 'S').

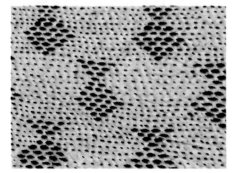

▲ Ghoti (brass pitcher carried by holy men).

▲ Pankha (fan).

▲ Koshi (water pitcher).

▲ Rosogulla (Bengali sweet).

▲ Pradeep (lamp).

▲ Bilai Powthi (cat's paw).

▲ Chokh (eye).

▲ Pukur chandi (ripples in a pond).

▲ Sitadul Phaansh (custard apple).

▲ Bhanga Kuina (broken elbow).

▲ Peper Patta (papaya leaf).

▲ Clip.

▲ Bansh Patta (bamboo leaf).

▲ Projapati (butterfly).

3. Holbein Stitch and Variations

Kantha embroidered with Holbein stitch showcase a rich diversity of patterns. Each pattern is named imaginatively to represent a highly abstract and stylised interpretation of objects and ideas, for instance *rail patti* signifies patterns inspired by train tracks, while *golak dhandi* is inspired by a maze.

When I visited kantha embroiderers in Katna village, they showed me many different styles of kantha with great pride and joy, including botanical kantha with stylised floral motifs, Holbein-stitched kantha with grid-like patterns and *phansher* kantha with detached chain stitches. They had embroidered many of the kantha themselves, while others had been inherited from their mothers and grandmothers. Many of the women work for the local cooperative, making kantha to earn an income. However, they also continue to make kantha for everyday use and to give as gifts for their family.

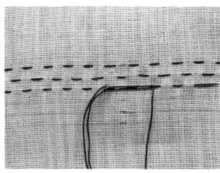

1 Draw six horizontal lines with an erasable pen, 5mm (¼in) apart or as desired. Number them 1 to 6. Stitch lines 1 to 3 with running stitch, using alternating stitch placement.

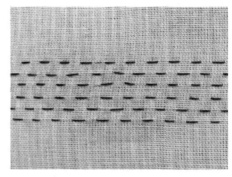

2 For line 4, follow the same stitch placement as line 3. Stitch line 5 using running stitch, matching the placement of rows and spaces with line 2. Similarly, stitch line 6 using running stitch, matching the placement with line 4.

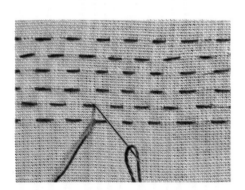

3 To start the pattern, make a vertical stitch from the left of a stitch on line 6 to right of the stitch directly

above on line 5. Continue this vertical running stitch line, joining lines 6 to 5, lines 4 to 3, lines 2 to 1.

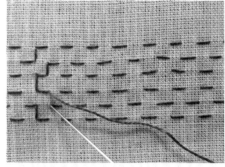

4 Make a second vertical line from lines 2 to 3 and lines 4 to 5.

◀ This large ancestral kantha has been embroidered by Jahanara Bibi entirely in Holbein stitches. It is brought out on ceremonial occasions in the household. From Katna, Murshidabad.

▶ Detail of the ancestral kantha (opposite) showing Holbein stitch.

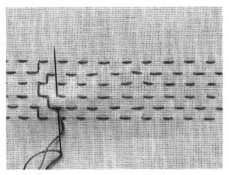

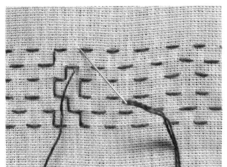

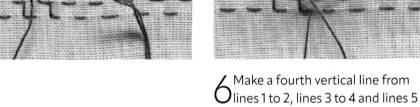

5 Make a third vertical line from lines 6 to 5, lines 4 to 3 and lines 2 to 1.

6 Make a fourth vertical line from lines 1 to 2, lines 3 to 4 and lines 5 to 6.

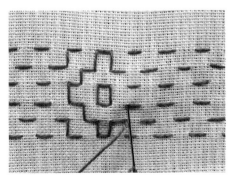

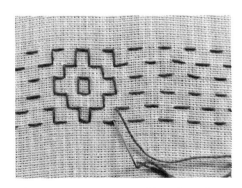

7 Make a fifth vertical line from lines 5 to 4 and lines 3 to 2.

8 Make a sixth vertical line from lines 1 to 2, lines 3 to 4 and lines 5 to 6.

9 Repeat steps 1–8 to create further motifs and continue the pattern.

Motifs and Patterns Using Holbein Stitch Variations

Holbein stitch is also called double running stitch. A wide range of patterns, including grids and chevrons, are created by working rows of running stitches and then filling the gaps with another running stitch.

Many kantha patterns made with Holbein stitch variations are similar to those seen in blackwork and Japanese sashiko. Several Bengali embroiderers refer to this as *hashia* stitch.

The kantha on these two pages have been embroidered by members of Street Survivors India, Katna, Murshidabad.

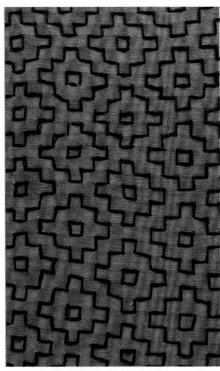

▲ Golok Dhandi (maze).

▲ Rail patti pattern, inspired by train tracks.

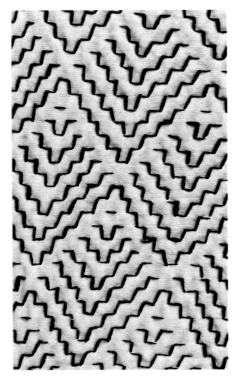

▲ Jhao (Christmas tree).

▲ Golok Dhandi (maze).

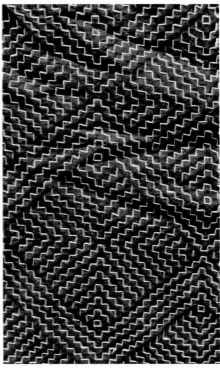

▲ Variation of Holbein stitches.

4. Kantha With Interlaced Stitches

When interlacing is applied across multiple rows of stitches, it creates intricate and complex patterns.

▲ Paddo kantha (lotus).

▲ Chosma (spectacles).

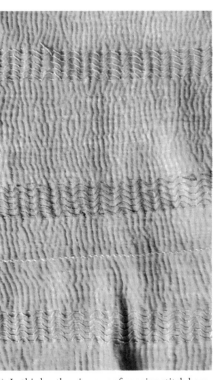

▲ In this kantha, six rows of running stitch have been interlaced in contrasting-colour threads to create distinct bands. Note the use of longer-length foundational running stitches compared to much shorter quilting stitches.

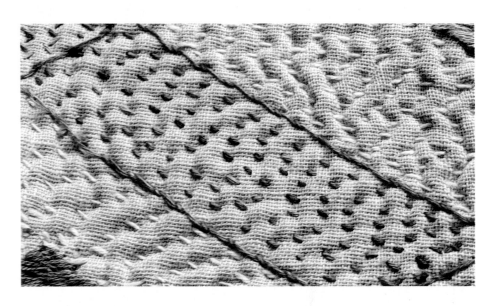

▶ Detail of a kantha showing interlaced running stitch.

Interlaced Running Stitch

Interlaced stitches range from simple to complex. As its simplest, a single row of running stitches is woven with another thread by passing it under each float of running stitch without going through the fabric. In the kantha tradition, myriad patterns are created by interlacing multiple rows of running stitches. These patterns are used to embellish borders or form overall patterns that cover the body of the kantha. The interlacing thread can be the same colour as the foundational running stitch or a contrast colour.

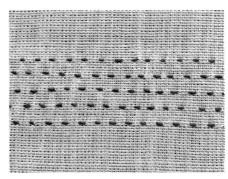

1 Draw five horizontal lines with an erasable pen, around 5mm (¼in) apart, and number them 1 to 5. Stitch lines 1 to 5 with running stitch, using alternating stitch placement. Keep the stitch size small.

2 Using a second thread in a contrast colour, emerge just above the first stitch on line 1. Insert your needle under the stitches starting from the first stitch of line 1 and moving diagonally left to line 5. Pull through.

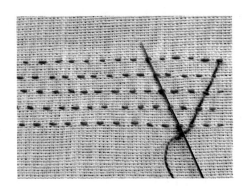

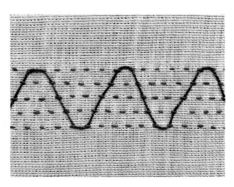

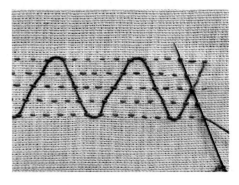

3 Insert your needle under the next stitch to the left in line 5, continue up diagonally towards line 1 and pull through. Check to ensure thread tension is the same throughout.

4 Change direction and continue interlacing in the same fashion until you reach the end of your stitched rows. Finish off with a knot on the reverse.

5 Begin the next interlacing stitch and emerge just under the first stitch on line 5, insert the needle under this stitch and continue diagonally up towards line 1. Pull through.

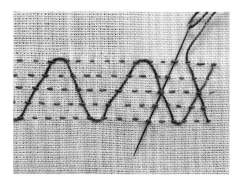

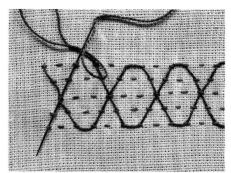

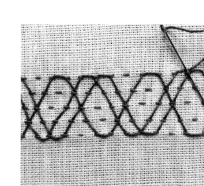

6 Continue interlacing in this manner until you reach the end of stitched lines.

7 Begin a third series of interlacements by bringing your needle out on the next stitch over from where you ended on step 6. Insert needle diagonally down towards line 5.

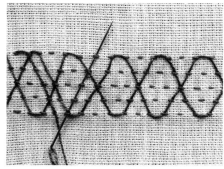

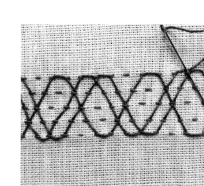

8 Change direction and continue interlacing from line 5 up to 1, then from line 1 down to 5, until you reach the end of the stitches on the right-hand side.

Myriad patterns are created by interlacing multiple rows of running stitches.

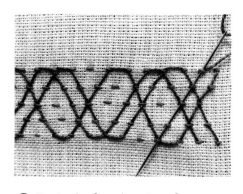

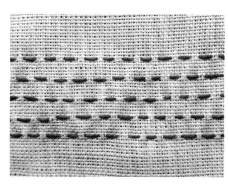

9 Begin the fourth series of interlacements by emerging just above the second stitch from the top right on line 1. Insert your needle diagonally down towards

line 5. Continue changing direction and interlacing until you reach the end of the stitches on the left-hand side.

10 Check the reverse side to ensure interlacing stitches have not gone through the fabric.

Stitches in Botanical Kantha from Katna

Botanical patterns in this style of kantha from Katna village are different to the ones I encountered in other kantha collections in India. These feature elegant floral designs in vivid colours, arranged in directional or overall patterns.

To me, the floral forms were reminiscent of the marble inlay work found in the Taj Mahal. In the eighteenth century, Murshidabad served as the capital of the Bengal Subah, the largest subdivision of the Mughal Empire encompassing the Bengal region, which includes modern-day Bangladesh, the Indian states of West Bengal, Bihar, Jharkhand and Odisha. The distinctive floral kantha patterns found in the region are thought to be influenced by the Mughal era.

The stitch vocabulary in this style of botanical kantha includes *mala* stitch or double chain stitch variations, herringbone stitch, convent stitch, Bokhara couching, *kadam phool* and running stitch for quilting.

◀ (*Overleaf*) Examples of interlaced stitch patterns embroidered by members of Street Survivors India, Katna, Murshidabad.

100

 Flower vines embroidered with Kashmiri stitch on an indigo background, quilted with running stitches. Courtesy of Street Survivors India, Katna, Murshidabad.

▶ Botanical kantha with a quilted white background, featuring elegant vines and flowers in vibrant colours. Courtesy of Street Survivors India, Katna, Murshidabad.

Popular Floral Motifs

Other popular floral motifs in Murshidabad's kantha include the following (images courtesy of Street Survivors India, Katna, Murshidabad):

▲ Joba (*Hibiscus rosa-sinensis*) embroidered with Kashmiri stitch.

▲ Makorshar Jhaal (spider's web) embroidered with Kashmiri stitch and herringbone stitch.

▲ Gulab (rose) embroidered with Kashmiri stitch.

Kadam Phool

Neolamarckia cadamba, called *kadam* in Bengal or burflower-tree, is an evergreen native tropical tree. Its highly fragrant orange flowers blossom in dense, globe-shaped clusters. The flower features on kantha as a circular motif made with a combination of running stitch and clusters of long straight stitches.

▲ (*and opposite*) Kadam Phool kantha (kadam flower).

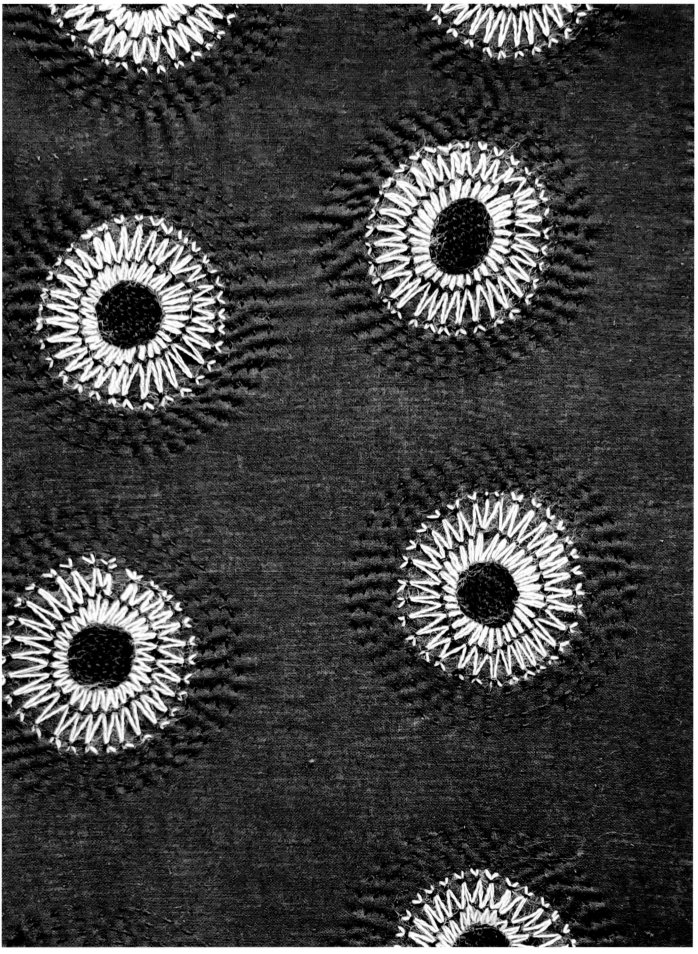

Border Stitches

Border patterns, called *par*, are embroidered around kantha in designs that imitate woven sari borders. Distinctive patterns are worked in bands along the edges of kantha, and sometimes also around the central focal motif in a square or rectangular frame.

The *par tola* style of kantha employs border designs in the field of the kantha, worked in vertical bands along the length or as concentric squares or rectangles around a central lotus motif, with trees of life or paisleys at the corners.

Stitches used to create border bands include: pattern darning (filling, grid, chevron, diagonal bands and circular), running stitches and interlaced stitches.

▷ Bands of borders.

(*Opposite left, top and bottom*) Kantha with borders embroidered with pattern darning stitches.

(*Opposite right*) Eight different border designs embellish this kantha. Collection of The Museum and Art Gallery, The Ramakrishna Mission Institute of Culture, Gol Park, Kolkata.

Kantha

Quilting Stitches

Quilting of the ground is done in numerous styles. While the most common method involves parallel rows of running stitches following the contours of the motifs, other styles can be observed, such as filling the ground with concentric squares, triangles or circles worked in running stitch, or parallel rows of running stitches that stretch from one end of the kantha to the other. Regardless of the quilting technique used, the quilting stitch passes through all layers of the kantha.

Kantha Stitch

Kantha stitch, a widely used quilting method, involves stitching parallel rows of running stitches that follow the contours of the motifs. The stitches are small in size with a longer gap between them, and the placement of stitches in consecutive rows is staggered rather than identical, giving the kantha surface a dotted appearance and its characteristic rippled effect.

Anne Morrell, in her book *Techniques of Indian Embroidery*, highlights the diversity in stitch length while quilting. She notes, 'The quilt can be worked with an evenly spaced stitch so that it is identical on either side, or with a long stitch on the side facing the embroiderer and a short stitch on the reverse side.' Kantha stitch for quilting is often worked in a colour that matches the base cloth, but is occasionally worked in a contrast colour.

In my discussions with embroiderers spanning different generations, I learnt that there is no definitive method of quilting kantha. Embroiderers may choose to quilt by following contours of motifs for some of their kantha; for others they opt to use multiple quilting techniques in the same piece, depending on various factors, such as the size of the area and their artistic inclination.

Many embroiders remarked that the quilting stitches reflect their moods – something that, as an artist, I identify with easily. I find the free-spirited approach to kantha making, as a powerful vehicle for the artistic expression of women's ability to hold their work lightly and follow their inner artistic voice, to be both inspiring and liberating.

106

Examples of Quilting Stitch Styles

▲ This example illustrates quilting stitches in the ground worked following the contours of the motifs.

▲ This sample shows diverse quilting styles in the ground, including rows and squares in the same piece.

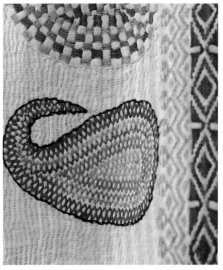

▲ Here, parallel rows of running stitches quilt the ground. The stitch is short and the gap between stitches is longer. Stitches in consecutive rows follow the placement in the previous row.

▲ Quilting stitches follow concentric rectangular shapes in the ground.

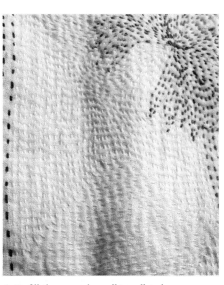

▲ To fill the ground, small tessellated squares are worked from the periphery towards the centre.

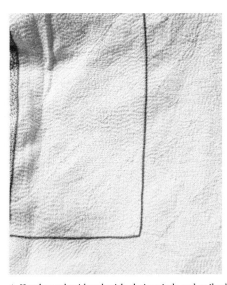

▲ Kantha embroidered with chain stitch and quilted with concentric forms, following the rhombus.

I find the free-spirited approach to kantha making, as a powerful vehicle for the artistic expression of women's ability to hold their work lightly and follow their inner artistic voice, to be both inspiring and liberating.

▶ (*Opposite*) Here, tone-on-tone quilting stitches follow the contours of the motifs.

▶ (*Top*) Quilting in tessellated rhombuses with the outline in worked in chain stitch and the quilting in running stitch.

▶ (*Bottom*) Quilting in semicircles.

▼ Quilting in concentric circles. Note how the space between adjacent circles is stitched following the contours of the circles.

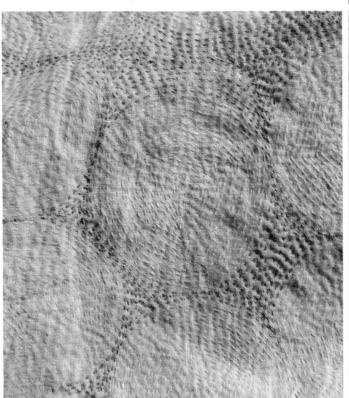

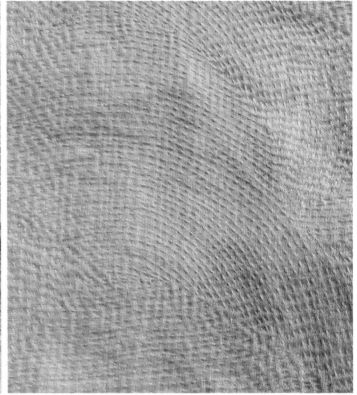

Construction

Pragmatic Layers

In rural Bengal, life flowed in sync with the rhythm of the seasons. The time of year dictated festivals, weddings and the planting and harvesting of crops. Living in sync with seasonal rhythms also meant there were periods when women had more time available to devote to kantha making. Traditionally, women made kantha during the monsoons, when the land was under water and they were at home, away from the fields. As Darielle Mason observed, making kantha was a slow labour of love: 'It took anywhere from six months to three generations to make a kantha.'

Niaz Zaman notes, in *The Art of Kantha Embroidery*, that the type of climate influenced the choice of cloth and number of layers used.

In turn, this determined the thickness of kantha, which influenced the type of stitches and motifs used. Northern areas of West Bengal and Bangladesh experience harsher winters compared to the southern parts, and so the cloth used in northern towns like Rajshahi was thicker than that used in southern towns like Jessore. Usually between five and seven layers of saris or dhotis were layered and stitched together to make kantha for winter, while two to three layers were used for lightweight summer kantha.

Shabnam Ramaswamy shared with me that up to eleven layers of cloth were sewn together for kantha that were intended to be used as mattresses on beds. Since the dexterity of the needle is reduced with an increase in the thickness of cloth and number of layers, the kantha embroidered in the northern region employed thicker stitches and simple repetitive patterns, while the southern regions used shorter stitch lengths and a wider range of patterns as they used a lighter cotton and fewer layers. Anne Morrell confirmed, 'The thicker the cotton or number of layers, the coarser the embroidery.'

Contemporary kantha I encountered on my field trip to West Bengal in 2022 were being made using three layers – often cotton or silk on top, a layer of light calico in the middle, followed by a layer of fine *mulmul* or voile. Having said that, a large number of contemporary kantha are made using only a single layer of cloth, especially those intended to be saris, stoles and scarves, as opposed to quilts.

▼ *Bostani* kantha, with concentric bands of botanical patterns and animal motifs are arranged around a central square. Collection of National Crafts Museum, New Delhi.

Preparing the Layers

Traditionally, to begin making kantha, discarded cloth was sorted into groups according to its condition – the worn-out, fragile fabrics were used for the inner layers, while those in relatively good condition were used to make the top and bottom layers. If the kantha was intended as a wedding gift, brand-new or newer cloth was used for the top layer.

Fabrics came from members of the same household and were viewed as blessings. Traditionally women's saris, and men's dhoti and lungis were used to make kantha. 'However, this is not the case today in the villages and cooperatives where pieces are produced using new fabric for tourists, trade and export', notes Anne Morrell.

Following the sorting, the woven sari borders and *pallu* (sari end-pieces) were removed from the lengths and ends. Some of these woven borders were later applied to the kantha edges, while others were used to draw out coloured and white threads for embroidery and stitching. However, this practice of using drawn-out threads for embroidery is no longer followed, and new threads are used for quilting and embroidery.

During our conversation, Shabnam Ramaswamy, the founder of Street Survivors India, shared that the women used the length of a hand as a unit of measurement, measuring the fabric from the tips of the fingers to the elbow. However, this practice changed when they began to make kantha for commercial contexts rather than domestic use, and they adopted standardised measurements for coverlets and bedspreads.

Traditionally, smaller cloth pieces were sewn together with close running stitches to make a larger piece of fabric for the top and bottom layers. The seam allowances were then pressed open so they lay flat. Next, the layers were ironed using a flat brass pitcher holding hot coals (before electric irons became readily available). The base layer was spread out on the earthen floor, often in the courtyard, and carefully stretched to ensure no wrinkles or folds remained in the cloth. Often this required more than one woman to work, so friends and neighbours were called upon to help at this stage. Smaller pieces, salvaged from worn-out saris, dhotis and lungis, formed the innermost layer. These were laid side by side on the base layer to create the required size. Finally, the top layer was laid to cover the inner layer(s).

Women used what was locally available to fashion into tools. In the old days they used thorns (*Khejur kanta*) of the date palm tree (*Phoenix sylvestris*), which grows abundantly in the region, to hold the layers together. Corners of the layered cloth were pinned to the mud flooring so as to keep the layers in place and the cloth stretched as the women began to stitch. Weights were also placed on the four corners to keep the layers straight. Nowadays, pearl pins and safety pins are used for securing layers before basting.

Marking Designs on Cloth

Women created their designs from memory and imagination. First, the central and corner motifs were established, followed by the borders, and then the ground was filled with a wide variety of motifs arranged in a whimsical manner. Particular emphasis was laid upon border designs.

In the past, women used colourants available at home to draw their designs on cloth, such as *holud gola* (turmeric paste), *alta* (a red dye made of lac applied to adorn the hands and feet) or a blue colourant used for laundry whitening. They drew freehand directly onto the cloth using a twig dipped in the liquid colourant. Later, this practice was replaced by the use of pencil or chalk.

Today, besides these tools, other methods of marking the cloth are prevalent, for instance the prick and pounce transfer method or tracing the drawing on the cloth (discussed in this section). However, the traditional practice of embroidering from memory and intuition continues, as I observed at Katna village and Kolkata.

The Prick and Pounce Transfer Method

The design is drawn on acetate paper or a heavier tracing paper, and pricked with a needle to create a series of small perforations along the drawn lines. Next, the perforated acetate sheet is placed over the embroidery fabric and a chalk powder is rubber over it to transfer the design.

In India, this method is modified slightly, and instead of the dry chalk powder, a solution is prepared by mixing powdered chalk, charcoal or blue fabric colourant with a quick evaporating liquid such as white petrol or kerosene oil. This chalk solution is then gently rubbed with a pounce over the acetate sheet, transferring the design onto the cloth. This method enables the design to be transferred accurately onto the cloth. Also, the acetate sheet can be used repeatedly, thus making it a popular choice for the cooperatives and ateliers.

Traditionally, dry pounce powder is pushed through the perforations using a pounce pad. However, the improvised practice of dissolving the pounce powder in a volatile liquid that evaporates at room temperature means that the design stays on the fabric much longer during the embroidery process and does not require repeated transfers as frequently as dry pounce powder. Dark powder is used on light-coloured fabrics, while white powder is used on dark fabrics.

Drawing Freehand

The design is drawn freehand onto the fabric
using a pencil, chalk or heat- or water-erasable
pens. I use a heat-erasable pen for drawing
my designs.

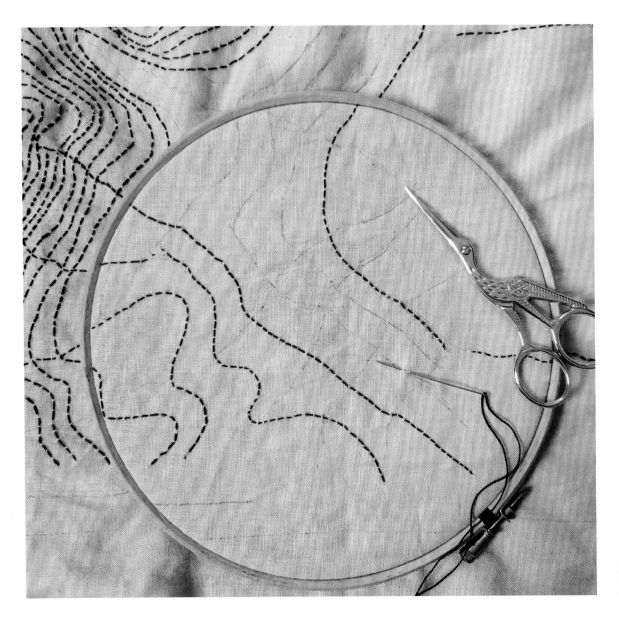

◀ Design drawn
freehand on the
fabric using heat-
erasable pen.

Transfer by Tracing

For transferring designs from paper to fabric, I suggest using a light box. Place the design onto the light box and tape it down to ensure it does not get displaced during the tracing process. Then place your fabric over the drawing and trace over it using a heat-erasable pen. This method works well for light to medium weights in light colours.

Transfer by Printing

Designs can be printed on fabric by screen printing, heat transfer or digital printing.

Transfer Using Dressmakers' Carbon Paper

Dressmakers' carbon papers can be a useful tool in transferring your drawings onto fabric, especially dark-coloured fabrics. They are available in a range of colours including white, yellow and red.

To use this method, lay the fabric flat, ensuring there are no creases, then place the dressmakers' carbon paper and finally the drawing over it. Ensure that the layers are pinned together so they do not get displaced during the drawing process. Next, run a blunt-tipped pencil or a roller pen over the design lines to transfer it onto the fabric. Avoid using a tracing wheel, as it can damage the paper and the fabric.

◀ This design has been printed onto the fabric in preparation for embroidery.

The Embroidery Process

Embroidery begins in the centre and is worked outwards. This ensures that the texture remains even. First, the central medallion is embroidered, followed by the corners, motifs, borders and finally, the ground. The edges are folded, turned in and stitched using a running stitch. Parallel rows of long basting stitches are stitched across the length and width, every few inches, in a grid format that holds the layers together. The basting stitches also act as a guide for embroidery.

The background is embroidered with small running stitches, stitched through all the layers. The smaller running stitch is referred to as *guri run* colloquially – *guri* means 'tiny' and *run* is shortened from running stitch. As Shabnam Ramaswamy told me, 'amongst the kantha embroiderers, quilting stitches are deemed good quality when they are "*maccher deem theke chhoto*", smaller than fish eggs.' For filling the ground, stitches are worked in small sections and are placed in concentric shapes, following the contours of motifs.

In many kantha pieces I studied in Murshidabad, the length of the quilting stitch is the identical to the distance between stitches, while in others, the stitch length is much smaller than the distance between them. After the first row of stitches is made, stitches in the following rows are placed such that the stitch length corresponds to a gap in the previous row, like brickwork. This placement is referred to colloquially as *pete-pete shilai*, roughly translated to consecutive rows of stitches placed in the 'stomach' of the sewing, or an alternate placement.

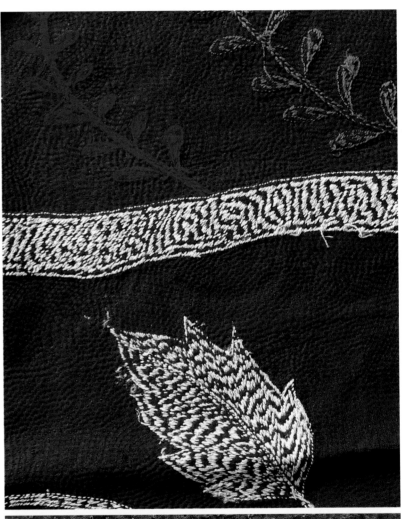

▶ (*Top*) Quilting follows the contours of the motifs.

▶ (*Bottom*) Quilting stitch detail.

Threads for Kantha Embroidery & Quilting

In the past, white cotton threads drawn from saris or garments were used for quilting the background, and coloured threads – often red, blue and black – from woven sari borders were used to embroider motifs and border patterns in kantha. Materials available locally were incorporated imaginatively. According to Anne Peranteau, crimped threads observed in the kantha embroidery of the Kramrisch and Bonovitz collections indicate that the strands were pulled apart from a plied thread to give a thicker appearance to the embroidered line. To me, the embroiderer's decision to seek an unusual thread in this instance evidences her creativity and openness to trying new materials.

As a wider range of yarns and colours became available, women incorporated them into their kantha. A range of materials was and is used to make kantha, not restricted to recycled cloth and threads. The base cloth can be a plain or patterned cotton, silk or cotton blend. Nowadays, cotton floss threads and perle are used in a wide range of colours for quilting the background, as well as for motifs and borders. During my research, I also came across more recent examples of kantha where twisted silk threads and acrylic wool have been used for embroidery.

Needles

In West Bengal, the most commonly used needles for kantha making are Pony Sharps, sizes 8, 9 and 10.

▲ Edges finished with binding.

Finishing Edges

A few different edge finishes can be observed in kantha. The vast majority of historical kantha have knife-edge finishing, rather than a binding. The design finishes about 1cm (⅜in) away from the edges, which are then turned inwards and stitched over. Edges in contemporary kantha are finished with one of the following methods:

1   Turning the seam allowance to the reverse, folding to 1cm (⅜in) and hemming

2   Bias binding

3   Double fold binding with mitred corners

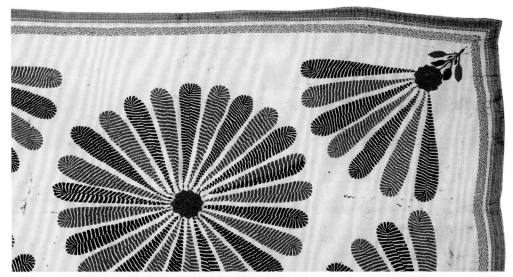

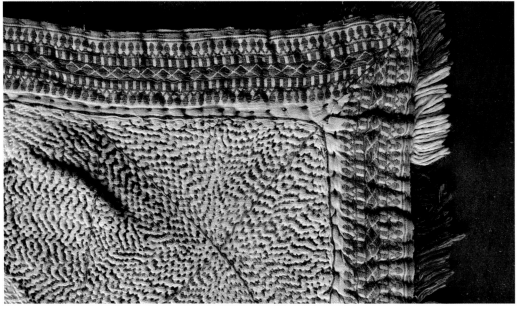

◁ (*Top*) Knife-turned edges, finished with blanket stitch detail. Collection of the National Crafts Museum, New Delhi.
(*Middle*) Woven borders attached at the edges of the kantha front. Collection of the National Crafts Museum, New Delhi.
(*Bottom*) Edges decorated with fringes. Collection of Street Survivors India, Katna, Murshidabad.

▶ Examples of folding the seam allowance to the reverse and finishing raw edges with hemming. Kantha embroidered by Hushnohana, Kolkata.

The Kantha Making Process

The method describes the kantha-making steps followed by members of Street Survivors India.

1 The fabric pieces are cut, pinned and basted together to make the required size of the kantha.

2 The pieces are joined together to make the ground cloth using a sewing machine. In the past, this was sewn by hand.

3 The first layer is laid flat and stretched, and weights are placed at the corners to stabilise the fabric.

4 Next, the fabric is ironed to remove any creases. All the seams are opened and the seam allowances are ironed flat.

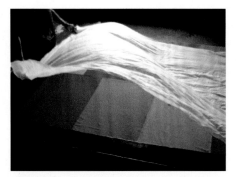

5 A layer of lightweight cotton is laid on the first layer.

6 This layer is stretched to match the first layer and ironed.

7 Fabric pieces are laid on the middle layer to form the third layer. The third layer can also be a whole cloth.

8 The pieces are basted to form a complete third layer. All three layers of kantha are tacked using long basting stitches, made in a grid.

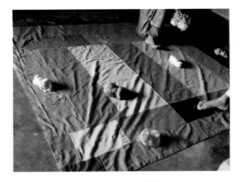

9 Threads are selected for embroidery, and then the embroidery and quilting are done.

10 Measurements often change after quilting, so the kantha is laid flat again, straightened and measured.

Corners are squared off, and any excess fabric is cut off and edges are straightened.

11 The raw edges are finished with bias binding.

12 Kantha are washed and dried in the sun.

◀ Border fragments possibly salvaged from another kantha have been used as a patch to reinforce worn-out sections along the edges of this kantha. Collection of the National Crafts Museum, New Delhi.

Repair

Repair, restitution and reinvention are integral to kantha. Kantha were repaired and cared for by the women in the family. Torn and worn-out sections were patched and mended, embroidered upon and quilted. When a kantha became too fragile to be mended, sections of it were salvaged to make smaller-sized kantha items, such as coin purses, or parts were used to patch and reinforce other kantha. Kantha were used in some form until they fell apart, after which time they were turned into rags and ultimately, when the rags were no longer workable, they were returned to the earth.

▷ Adding patches is a common method of repair in kantha.

▽ (*Left*) A piece of another kantha is stitched to the quilt crudely to mend a (possibly) torn section.

▽ (*Right*) A kantha drying in the sun shows a patch with turned-over edges used to mend a worn-out section.

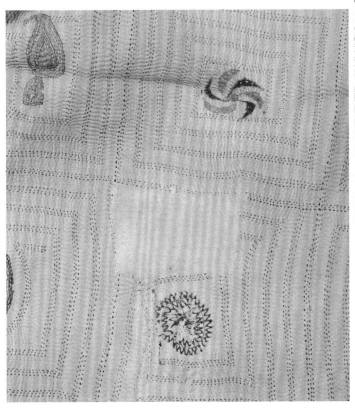

Reimagining Tradition

The influence of kantha has crossed borders and cultures, inspiring artists, makers and designers to reimagine tradition across the globe. My hope is that the diverse approaches highlighted in this chapter will seed new thoughts and inspire you to develop your own unique ways of reusing, repurposing, reflecting and refocusing towards a more creative, slower, more thoughtful art practice and life.

A Sense of Place

Sense of place refers to the emotional attachment that we have to a particular location. It is the feeling of being connected to a place in a deep and meaningful way, and it can be influenced by a wide range of factors, including geography, history, culture and personal experiences. Sights, sounds and smells can contribute to a person's sense of place, as can their memories and associations with that location. Sense of place is important because it helps to create a sense of identity and belonging for individuals and communities.

Kantha are potent documents of a sense of place. They present nuanced narratives of the lived experiences of women in a particular place and time. Kantha motifs often feature images of local flora and fauna as well as scenes from daily life and commentary on contemporary events, which serve as a record of the cultural and environmental context in which the women who created them lived. Thus, stitches become a window into personal and collective histories. For me, the stitched marks I make on cloth are segues into conjuring up personally meaningful places.

My piece, *House of Belonging*, seeks to explore the meaning of home. Stitching the contours of familiar streets of Delhi on fragments of cotton dyed with Indian indigo, was an act of remembering a period in my life when home was a clearly defined place in a city that felt mine, before the definition of home became more transient as a consequence of my move to the UK.

Now that I live in London, the act of stitching a Delhi map is a way for me to revisit my city as I remember it, which perhaps now exists only in my memory, as contemporary Delhi differs greatly from what I remember of the city. Constructing the base cloth from fragments alludes to fragments of memories coming together to make the fabric of life. Mapping memories and my sense of displacement through stitch feels cathartic. Like the kantha embroiderers who came before me, I am using the language of textiles to tell stories of place and belonging.

▼ Ekta Kaul, *House of Belonging* (2023), 58 × 58cm (23 × 23in).

Interview № 1
Dorothy Caldwell

Dorothy Caldwell is an American-born Canadian fibre artist known for her abstract printed and stitched textiles. Dorothy's work has been exhibited widely and is included in permanent collections at The Museum of Art and Design, New York City; The International Quilt Museum, Lincoln, Nebraska; the Museum of Fine Arts, Boston; The Canadian Museum of History, Hull, Quebec; and others.

I encountered Dorothy's work first online as a student and then in the flesh several years later and on every occasion I remember being struck by its electrifying presence.

EK: Tell me a little bit about your childhood and how you first became interested in stitch.
DC: From a very young age, art was what I did. My parents were creative, and we made things together as a family. Quilts made by my grandmother and great-grandmother were on our beds. My mother often pointed out individual pieces of cloth, saying, 'this is from a dress that I wore in high school' or 'this was from my father's shirt'. It seemed as if family was sewn into the quilts.

Later, I studied painting and printmaking. At that time – the late sixties and early seventies – minimalism was at its height, and in art school we looked at painters such as Frank Stella, Ellsworth Kelly and Donald Judd. At the time, it didn't occur to me that stitching or other textile practices could be art.

Around the same time, my mother took me to see the Jonathan Holstein quilt exhibition at The Whitney in New York. I was struck by how these quilts, made by anonymous women fifty to one hundred years earlier, paralleled and even surpassed the paintings of the contemporary minimalist artists. It was the first time I saw textiles as art.

▼ *Fjord* (2011–12), 2.5 × 2.6m (8 ft 5in × 8 ft 6in), wax and silkscreen resist on cotton with applique and stitching.

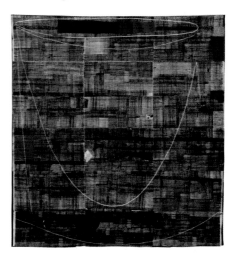

EK: What are the themes that you explore in your work?
DC: I have a strong image of the backyard of the house I lived in until the age of five. I remember the placement of the fence, trees, bushes and flowers clearly. Around the perimeter was the cherry tree, then the pear and the plum tree. As you followed the fence around the border you came to the pussy willows, then the blue morning glories growing on the fence. These were my landmarks, all happening in a square shape. I knew this landscape intimately.

This early childhood memory has evolved into looking at the ongoing picture of 'movement through' and 'living in' a landscape. I am interested in human marks: the grid layout of cultivated land and its interaction with the natural geology.

Each night, when I leave the studio, I stop to look at the Pole Star. It is another constant that places me in my world. These shapes and forms are the repeated reference marks in my work. When I'm in an unfamiliar place, I look for the geological forms that set the stage and then focus on the intimate textures underfoot or details that can be physically touched.

EK: What materials and processes do you use in your work?
DC: The base material, cotton or

◀ Dorothy Caldwell (born Bethesda, Maryland, USA, 1948).

▶ *After The Robins Return* (2019), 42 × 42cm (16.5 × 16.5in).

linen, is textured through silkscreen printing, batik and block printing. This fabric is then constructed into a large-scale background that is worked on with appliqué and kantha-like stitching.

EK: When did you first encounter kantha? Which particular aspects of kantha do you find inspiring and how are you exploring them within your work?

DC: During a residency researching the quilt collection in Quebec, Stephen Inglis, then head of the museum, handed me an article on kantha stitching. When I read it, what struck me was the idea that kantha was an art form that had evolved out of everyday domestic practices of mending and repair. The base was reconstructed from fragments of old white saris and dhotis – cloth that had a previous life. Furthermore, it said that the blue and red threads of the selvedge edges were unwoven and used to make coloured stitches on the white background.

Something about this touched me: that women would take the time to unweave the selvedges just to have something beautiful to stitch with. The cloth fragments and threads were used to construct something entirely new, while at the same time these materials retained something

of their previous history. It was reminiscent of other formal textile art forms that evolved out of mending and recycling old cloth: Japanese *sashiko*, and North American quiltmaking. It is at the juncture when cloth is worn out and no longer useful that women had the opportunity to express their creativity and make something that was their own.

In 1997, I researched the rich collections at the Asutosh Museum of Indian Art and the Gurusaday Museum in Kolkata, which housed rich collections of kantha. I also visited the Calico Museum in Ahmedabad to see exquisite examples of old kantha, as well as several stitching cooperatives in Kolkata, West Bengal, where I saw accomplished stitching and economically successful work. My travels took me to Bihar, where I

learnt about the tradition of sujani, which is similar to kantha in its ethos of storytelling through stitch on repurposed cloth.

This 1997 research trip to India influenced my decision to include stitching in my work. The layering of cloth, reconstruction in sujani and kantha from used saris and dhotis and intensive stitching as a 'drawing' line all were admirable qualities that I have made part of the repertoire of marks in my work.

Having studied painting and printmaking, I can't help but think of the kantha stitch as a mark like any other mark: a dot or a line or a texture. I like the aspect of time in kantha. The stitches are built over time as if each stitch is a second. Stitching records time into cloth.

dorothycaldwell.com

Textural Landscapes

Texture is a fundamental aspect of our sensory experience, and it plays a vital role in our emotional and physical well-being. Research has shown that our need for texture and physical touch is innately biological, and goes beyond basic survival instincts.

A famous study conducted by Harry Harlow in the 1950s demonstrated the importance of texture for baby rhesus monkeys. In the study, baby monkeys were given a choice between two surrogate 'mothers' – one made of wire and the other covered in soft terry cloth. Both were given a milk bottle at different times. When only the wire mother provided a source of food, the baby monkeys came to feed but immediately returned to the soft, textured terry cloth mother for comfort and security.

Humans, too, have a deep-seated emotional response to tactility. One of our first sensorial experiences as newborns is the touch of our mother's skin and the feel of a soft swaddling blanket. Texture not only plays a significant role in our enjoyment of the world around us as visual or gustatory stimuli, it evokes emotion in an elemental way too.

Kantha attests to this dual quality of texture; tactility is an integral part of its visual appeal as well as its emotional significance. The feeling of being wrapped in the soft layers of cloth that once held the bodies of loved ones is a powerful source of comfort. The soft, rippled surface and stitched rhythms speak of the love and care that was poured into making the kantha. To be wrapped in kantha feels like being embraced by absent mothers and grandmothers.

In this section we will discuss how contemporary artists and designers are pushing the boundaries of this traditional craft by experimenting with texture in creative ways. I hope the perspectives shared in this section will encourage you to explore how texture can be a powerful tool for artistic expression and create tactile works that are visually interesting and emotionally resonant.

Playing With Fabric Shrinkage

Unlike most embroidery techniques that simply embellish the surface, kantha stitches fundamentally change the form of the textile, sculpting it into delicate ripples or dramatic ridges, which I find really exciting. To me, the white-on-white often used to quilt the base cloth feels like a tranquil counterpoint to the exuberant motifs. Playing with the contrast and techniques that heighten the texture can be a powerful way of evoking emotions and creating sensorial experiences through cloth.

Texture can be created in several ways besides stitch placement. One of the techniques I really enjoy is to quilt two or more fabrics that have different rates of shrinkage. In the example you see below, I have stitched together two fabrics with different shrinking rates and soaked them in warm water. Both fabrics shrink differently, creating a rippled texture.

You can experiment with quilting:

- A loosely woven fabric with a tightly woven fabric

- A cotton or linen with a synthetic blend like polycotton

- Wool with cotton or zero shrinkage fabrics like polyester.

▼ Detail of *Zen Garden* (Ekta Kaul, 2020, 21 × 29cm [8.2 × 11.4in]) showing texture achieved through differential shrinkage.

▼ Detail of abrasion layers.

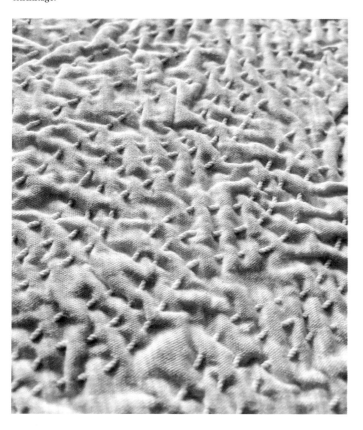

Abrasion

You can layer two or three fabrics and quilt them together to create interesting abraded surfaces by gently rubbing the top layer with a soft-grade sandpaper so it reveals the layers underneath. Layering contrasting colours can result in dramatic effects, but playing with tone-on-tone can be rewarding too.

Interview № 2
Santanu Das (Maku Textiles)

Santanu Das is known for his nuanced textiles and slow fashion sold through discerning stores around the world under the label Maku. Santanu trained at the National Institute of Design, Ahmedabad, and later spent time working in the US. Upon returning to India, Santanu established Maku Textiles with a manifesto of creating sustainable fashion, using time-honoured methods and the exceptional craft skills of India. Creating bespoke woven and embroidered textiles in a restrained palette of shades of indigo, Santanu explores textures in innovative ways.

When I visited Santanu's atelier in Kolkata, we discussed his love of kantha textures and how its tactility inspires him.

EK: Can you share your early influences and what sparked your interest in kantha?
SD: Kantha has always been a part of my childhood. My grandmother quilted and made kantha in her spare time using recycled fabrics. I remember the annual ritual of kantha being brought out before *durga puja* in the winters and laid on the terrace to soak up the sunshine. In our family, like in many other Bengali families, kantha were never bought but rather stitched as a labour of love and passed on to loved ones.

EK: Can you describe the inspirations that drive your work?
SD: My inspiration comes from my memories and personal experiences. I seek to express myself through materials and techniques in fabric.

EK: I am so intrigued by your materials and processes. Can you tell me more about them?
SD: My creative process is driven by playing with materials and learning by doing. We began to explore kantha at our studio about six years ago. It started as a simple enquiry:

▼ Detail of Latukika.

How could I incorporate wool into Indian textiles in an exciting way and create innovative surfaces that express my aesthetic?

Kantha quilting with wool seemed the immediate answer. And so we began to experiment with quilting silk and cotton with woollen threads; we boiled and felted them. This process completely transformed the quilted cloth, which I found really exciting. Since then, we have been using this technique to create richly textured quilted cloth and incorporate it into our fashion and accessories collections.

EK: You work in a restrained palette of natural indigo and whites only. What led to making this an essential part of your practice?
SD: Our world today is flooded with endless options, especially in fashion. I want to challenge this through my minimal approach. It is about reminding ourselves that by restricting our choices to fewer options, we create a more sustainable world. Working with indigo, supporting traditional skills and championing sustainable fabrics is part of my holistic approach to sustainability.

makutextiles.in

▶ (*Top*) Sigala.

▶ (*Bottom*) Kukkuta.

▼ Vaka.

Interview № 3
Stitch by Stitch

▲ Karen Sear Shimali (born Witney, Oxfordshire, England, 1966) and Graham Hollick (born Billericay, Essex, England, 1964), founders of Stitch by Stitch.

Stitch by Stitch was founded by British designer Graham Hollick after what he describes as several life-changing trips to India. Graham admits to feeling as though he must have lived in India in a past life, such is his feeling of affinity with the country.

Today, together with Karen Sear Shimali, Stitch by Stitch creates handmade and small-batch-produced textiles for residential interiors, working with artisan weavers, skilled embroiderers and quilt makers in Gujarat in India, Nepal and England. Their kantha quilts are skilfully executed by hand by a master quiltmaker in Gujarat, distinguishable by the tiny stitches in close, neat rows. The base cloth is Kala cotton, otherwise known as Old World cotton, which is an ancient, drought resistant species that has been grown in the region since 3000 BCE.

EK: Could you share your personal history, and how your fascination with stitching – particularly in the context of kantha – first began?
GH: I grew up in a household where my mother was a couture dressmaker, so I was always surrounded by textiles and sewing. My interest only grew stronger as I went on to study textiles and fashion at Winchester School of Art, where I met Karen.

Many years later I was invited to work on a project with SEWA (Self Employed Women's Association, the single largest women workers' central trade union in India) in Gujarat, India and this is where I discovered many embroidery techniques. I was introduced to our quilter Rhymal and his family. This is really where my love of kantha began.

Later, when I had already started Stitch by Stitch, I joined forces with Karen, and kantha quilts became an important part of our studio portfolio.

EK: Tell me about your creative process.
GH: We always start with the skills of the artisans themselves, then we look at how we can make them a little more contemporary and appealing to an interior design clientele in the UK and Europe. Much of what we do is with unbleached Kala cotton, both to show the beauty of the natural cloth but also to avoid using chemical dyes.

EK: What materials and processes do you use in your work?
GH: Most of our quilts and related cushions use the indigenous Gujarati Kala cotton, the reintroduction of which has been championed by the Kutch-based NGO Khamir.

Our master quiltmaker creates the quilts with tiny intricate stitches, honouring the tradition.

EK: Which aspects of kantha do you find inspiring and how are you exploring them within your work?
GH: We love the tradition of this stitch and also its simplicity. Looking beyond tradition, we like to experiment and explore where the stitch marks and textures can lead us. For instance, we have created a collection, layering image and texture by block printing a pattern based on a kantha stitch and then stitching it on top with a 'real' kantha stitch.

EK: What is the future of kantha, according to you?
GH: To me, kantha means a skill and an age-old tradition. I believe kantha is beyond trends. I therefore expect it to continue as a perennial in the world of handmade textiles.

stitchbystitch.uk

▲ Raw Chindi organic Kala cotton kantha quilt,
208 × 160cm (82 × 63in).

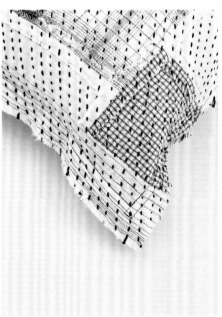

*Looking beyond
tradition, we like to
experiment and explore
where the stitch marks
and textures can lead us.*

▲ Chindi organic cotton patchwork quilt, 208 ×
160cm (82 × 63in).

▲ Detail of Raw Chindi patchwork kantha cushion,
60 × 40cm (24 × 16in).

Deconstruction, Reconstruction and Reincarnation

End of life in one form is only the start of a new one in another. I grew up in India imbibing this belief. The Indian way of life and Eastern philosophical traditions taught me that time and life are cyclical. I learnt that objects have an inherent ability to be repurposed at the end of their life cycle into new forms or avatars until they fall apart entirely and are returned to the earth.

My parents, both of whom were entomologists (insect scientists), taught us siblings to respect our planet's precious resources. While my father showed us rainwater harvesting and topsoil conservation at the university where they worked, my mother applied her scientific acumen to creating a biodiverse garden at home and taught us to repurpose domestic objects to avoid waste. From saving vegetable peels for our garden compost and reinventing leftovers into new recipes, to patiently unravelling the jumpers that my brother and I had outgrown, steaming them and re-knitting them into new designs, and saving old saris for making rag rugs and quilts, she led by example in being a thoughtful Earth citizen.

In India, an entire ecosystem of repair and recycling exists. Repair shops are ubiquitous, mending everything from kitchen appliances to zips in bags. Cobblers mend old shoes; *raffugars* or darners mend rips in saris and clothes. Old newspapers can be exchanged for cash, and discarded garments for new vessels. Thus, one is incentivised to recycle.

I remember the annual ritual of taking quilts to the local quilt shop just before the start of winter. The old quilt was opened up carefully and the cotton batting inside was taken out and laid in the sunshine. Then the batting would be beaten with a wooden mallet to remove any dirt and to fluff it up to restore softness and its ability to hold body heat. The top and bottom fabrics would be washed and darned. After this, the batting would be carefully placed back between the fabric layers and sewn together with running stitches. One could specify the weight of the quilt too, to make it suitable for the harsh North Indian winters or the mild springs. This traditional form of re-quilting continues to be practised widely in India, reaffirming older practices of preservation and renewal.

Deconstruction and reconstruction is a powerful way of repurposing old garments or fabrics by dismantling them and reconstructing them into something new. By unravelling, patching and embroidering discarded saris and fabrics, kantha breathes new life into them and transforms tattered fabrics into something new and even more beautiful than before.

In my opinion, kantha invites us to pause and fashion thoughtful, creative responses to the ageing process. Inspired by the traditional practice of unravelling threads from sari borders, I unravelled threads from my son's much-loved denims that he had outgrown. I used this thread to stitch my work *Always & Forever*, mapping memories of my own childhood and motherhood.

◀ The threads I unravelled from my son's denim jeans.

▼ Ekta Kaul, *Always and Forever* (2023) (58 × 58cm [23 × 23in]), made using retrieved threads from my son's denims.

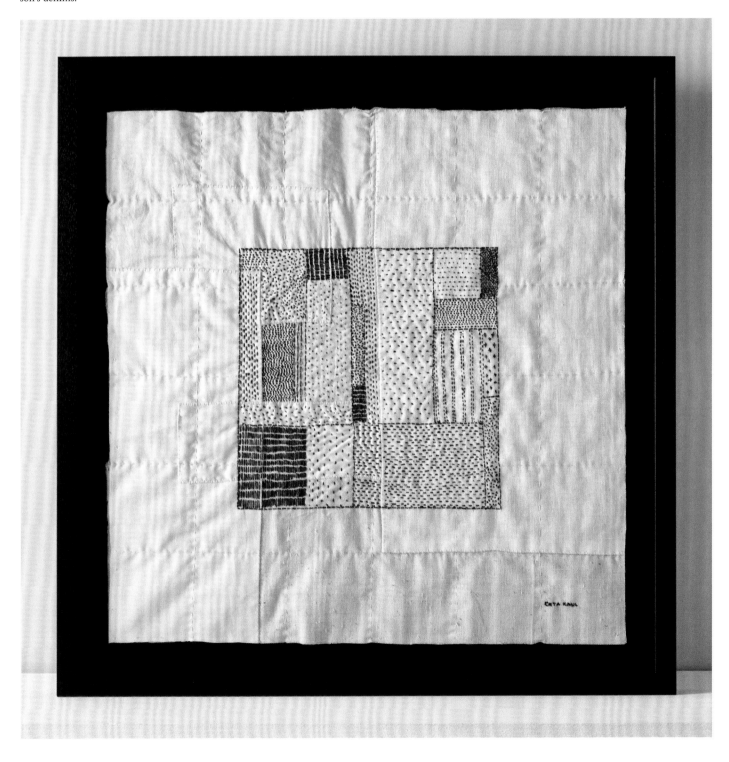

Interview № 4
Archana Pathak

Archana Pathak is an India-born, London-based textile artist. She works with found memory artefacts including old photographs, postcards, letters, diaries and maps. Through these, she contemplates the notion of home and belonging as well as the interplay of memory, place and identity.

EK: Tell me a little bit about your childhood and how you first became interested in stitching, especially in kantha.
AP: Growing up in India, I lived a bit of a nomadic life with my parents. My father was in the armed forces, and with each new posting I discovered new Indian towns and cities. Later in life, the pursuit of higher studies and work took me to new places in India and eventually to the UK, all of which continue to influence my work.

I was formally introduced to textiles and craft when I began studying at the National Institute of Design, Ahmedabad. However, Indian textiles and craft objects were part of my everyday life, even before going to design school. I remember my maternal grandmother's quilts in North India, called *gudris*, which she used to stitch using old textiles with simple running stitches.

Stitch returned to my life in a significant way while I was doing my master's degree in London as a new mother. Stitch gave me a contained approach to making, expressing and connecting to myself deeply and embarking on the journey of artmaking.

EK: Tell me about your practice and your creative process.
AP: My practice is of British and Indian heritage, and I specialise in stitch and fine art textiles. Through my collection of old found objects, like photographs, postcards, letters, diaries and maps, I explore the interplay of memory, place and identity. To me, old maps bring forth the evolving nature of boundaries – both physical and psychological – and are a metaphor for evolving identities. The collected artefacts inform my process and eventually take the form of the thread that I use.

EK: You use deconstruction and reconstruction so creatively in your work. Can you elaborate on your materials and processes?
AP: My making process is very simple and my tools are minimal. I love working with vintage linen, hemp and found objects. I heat-transfer images of artefacts onto a lightweight cotton fabric and then cut fine laces to create my thread. The stitch is primarily a running stitch.

EK: What does kantha mean to you?
AP: Kantha means simplicity and home for me. The reason I feel drawn to kantha is its ability to hold emotions. My work is driven by feelings and that is why kantha *gudri* resonates and touches me deeply.

EK: Tell me about your recent projects.
AP: One of my recent projects is 'Reimagined Landscapes: Memories of Being', a series of four pieces. It is made from a mix of collected old maps of places we know, lived in, travelled to, were displaced from or longed for. I created a mélange of threads made from these collected old maps to slow stitch and to render landscapes that are harmonious representations of coexistence, multiplicity and connectedness. It attempts to tap into the innocence of nature and interconnectedness. Inspired by the cycles of nature, a cycle of a day or change of seasons, the series is born out of the constant tussle to belong to a place or two… to get over the questions one has when one sees these landscapes. Where? Which place? Which country? To be able to see it as is.

EK: What are your hopes for the future?
AP: This quote by John Steinbeck: 'Just

◀ Archana Pathak
(born Lucknow, India,
1978) in her studio.

set one day's work in front of the last
day's work. That's the way it comes
out. And that's the only way it does.'
My hope is to be able to keep showing
up at my studio and be guided by the
process. I hope for a future where we
prioritise environmental concerns
and live harmoniously with nature.

**EK What advice would you give
someone who is just starting
with kantha?**
AP: Just start and be with it. Witness
what simplicity and meditative
repetition of this process can
unfold for you.

archanapathak.com

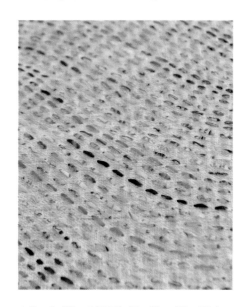

▲ My thread (2019).

▲ Detail of *Flow 1* (2020), 45 × 45cm (18 × 18in).

▲ *Reimagined Landscape* (2022), each 68 × 38cm (27 × 15in).

▲ *Core* (2021), 25cm (10in) diameter.

▲ Detail of *To Set* (2022), 68 × 38cm (26.7 × 15in).

Interview № 5
Abraham & Thakore

Abraham & Thakore is one of India's most respected design studios, known for their timeless fashion and textiles, rooted in a strong respect for material and traditional Indian craft, yet with a contemporary sensibility. The studio was initially established in 1992 by David Abraham and Rakesh Thakore, graduates of the National Institute of Design (NID), Ahmedabad, who were later joined by Kevin Nigli, a design graduate of the National Institute of Fashion Technology, New Delhi.

Their handmade collections are sold through luxury stores like The Conran Shop, Browns, Liberty, Selfridges and Harrods in London and Le Bon Marché in Paris, in addition to stores in India. The studio has been incorporating kantha alongside bespoke handwoven and handprinted textiles in their collections for decades, presenting fresh takes on tradition.

I spoke with David Abraham about kantha when I visited the studio in Delhi.

EK: When did you first become interested in kantha?
DA: I studied textile design at the NID, which exposed me to Indian textile traditions, of which kantha was one. Since establishing our design studio, kantha has been an important part of our collections.

EK: What materials and processes do you use in your work?
DA: I design fashion collections several times a year for Abraham & Thakore. I am interested in finding design solutions that are somehow connected to Indian clothing and our textile culture. We work with a large diversity of materials and techniques.

▲ Hand-embroidered kantha shirt and skirt with cotton and silk patchwork, and sequins made from discarded x-ray films.

◀ David Abraham
(born Singapore, 1955)
and Rakesh Thakore
(born Delhi, India,
1956).

*I believe that kantha is
an elegant and practical
solution to recycling,
with enormous design
potential.*

I believe that kantha is an elegant
and practical solution to recycling,
with enormous design potential. I am
especially inspired by kantha's facility
of patching textiles together with
hand stitching, in which the technique
of construction is also the decorative
element. Kantha features regularly in
our seasonal collections. We designed
a collection entirely focused on
recycling in 2015 called 'Assemble,
Disassemble, Reassemble' where
we explored kantha as a form of
recycling, incorporating textile waste
and offcuts from our studio.

**EK: What are your thoughts on the
future direction of kantha?**
DA: It has enormous potential in
the making of clothing and home
textiles in India, where exceptional
handcrafting skills are still available.

**EK: What are your hopes for
the future?**
DA: My hope for the future is that
we will learn to consume sensibly
and that beautiful handmade
products and objects will continue
to be made.

abrahamandthakore.com

▲ Offcuts kantha
kaftan, and texture
and stitch details.

▶ Sayan Chanda (born Kolkata, India, 1989).

Interview № 6
Sayan Chanda

Sayan Chanda is an India-born, London-based artist. He creates hybrid forms that conjure votive offerings, ritual markings and folk iconography using fibre, clay and articles of personal significance, like the kantha quilt.

He graduated with an MFA from Camberwell College of Art, London, before training at the National Institute of Design, Ahmedabad. Chanda had his first solo show at Jhaveri Contemporary, Mumbai, in October 2022.

He has exhibited his works at Commonage Projects, a project space in East London, and will be exhibiting as part of *Actions for the Earth* by Independent Curators International (a series of travelling exhibitions in the US), alongside works by Cecilia Vicuña, Ana Mendieta and Mithu Sen, among others. He undertook an artist residency in Senegal run by the Josef and Anni Albers Foundation in September 2023.

Chanda uses kantha as a source of inspiration as well as his raw material to create sculptural, hybrid forms.

EK: How have textiles shaped your creative journey?
SC: Kantha, jamdani and the gamchha were an integral part of my childhood in Kolkata, India. They were and still are an active, functional component of the indigenous material culture of Bengal and have had a deep influence on me. As ubiquitous as they were, their importance was brought out particularly during festivals, occasions and their role in rituals.

During the four invaluable years I spent studying textiles at the National Institute of Design, Ahmedabad, I was sensitised towards India's craft traditions and makers. My work has evolved by studying and experiencing folk and subaltern culture over the years and by working closely with traditional craftspeople in remote niches of India. I also factor in conversations on craft, gender, gatekeeping and museum collections of indigenous objects in the West.

EK: Can you tell me more about your practice?
SC: Employing laboured methods of tapestry weaving, stitching, dyeing, unpicking found textiles and hand building, I work intuitively, giving physical forms to my anxieties, mythologies, and individual and collective memory. My tapestries and fired clay objects often function as

▼ *Deity 7* (2020), unpicked quilt, cotton yarn, 48 × 36cm (19 × 14in).

Deity 3 (2020), unpicked quilt, handspun cotton, 57 × 35cm (22 × 14in).

Deity 5 (2020), unpicked quilt, cotton yarn, 54 × 31cm (21 × 12in).

▶ *Deity 14* (2021),
unpicked quilt,
cotton yarn,
76 × 30cm (30 ×
12in).

▲ *Nirrti 2* (2023), cotton cord, vintage quilt, sisal, dyed cotton, 198 × 150cm (78 × 59in).

Used vintage kantha are probably the most important material for me. I unpick old kantha, rearrange them into folds and stitch them. I also tear unpicked kantha into yarns, and dye and weave them as my weft.

EK: You attribute kantha as being the most significant material in your work. How does kantha inform your work?
SC: I work with materials with an inherent memory or narrative. Through unpicking and tearing the kantha, I enter into a conversation not just with the materials, but also with their makers, their personal mark-making and narratives, and I negotiate with the idea of ownership.

The hybrid objects that I make are representations of votives and ritual objects that I relate to deeply at a personal level. When an object becomes invested with emotion or intention, it transforms from a mere material object into a votive; and following the same reasoning, I consider kantha a ritual object.

My fascination with the past aligns with working with textiles, clay and especially vintage kantha quilts. They allow me to imagine that my hybrid objects are relics of a lost civilisation. Jasimuddin's beautiful lyrical poem 'Nakshi Kanthar Math' ('The Field of the

totems, portals and talismans, alluding to objects or moments in my past that still hold significance for me. At its core, my work investigates object-making as a form of personal and cultural expression.

EK: What materials and processes do you use in your work?
SC: I work primarily with fibre and vintage textiles and have recently taken up clay as a medium. I mostly use cotton yarn, some of which is handspun in Madhya Pradesh, India. I use sisal, jute and other natural fibres, all of which I hand dye and weave on simple makeshift frames at my London studio.

Embroidered Quilt') is one of my favourite poems.

EK: What does kantha mean to you?
SC: Kantha becomes a bridge to Kolkata, my childhood home and the objects and memories surrounding it. This bridge feels all the more meaningful now that I live in London. Kantha embodies familiarity, groundedness and the connections I have made to places and objects as a child.

Furthermore, the references and cultural contexts in my work draw from folk religiosity and have nothing to do with mass religion. One of the reasons I look towards folk religiosity for inspiration is how syncretic and human it feels. Kantha, to me, symbolises this very syncretism, which is visibly becoming rarer in today's world.

EK: In your *Deity* series and woven tapestries you incorporate kantha in such a potent way. Tell me more about these works.
SC: I first began working with kantha as an intuitive exercise to transform the quilts. My primary concern was the afterlife of intimate, culturally relevant objects. Unpicking used quilts and revealing layers of stitched fabric became a visceral and cathartic process for me. Twisting and folding them, stitching and embroidering the

thick layers almost felt like creating new narratives in the life of the quilt. The resultant pieces are almost like runes or alphabets of a lost fictional script, alluding to charms to ward off evil eye and the ritualistic repetition in making them. These investigations eventually turned into my *Deity* series.

I also use kantha as weft in my woven tapestries. I unpick the quilts, tear them by hand into thin strips, dye them and weave them into hybrid forms that conjure objects ranging from masks used in folk performances and aniconic representations of indigenous folk goddesses to votive objects offered in local shrines, among others. Kantha becomes the medium that helps me draw from these sources. Its usage might not be immediately apparent in the works, but on a closer look, one can see the frayed edges, the running stitches and the unpicked layers of the quilt peeking through. These quilts help me imbue each tapestry with a significance that might not be possible through using newer, more conventional materials.

EK: What can kantha teach us?
SC: I think the kantha quilt is gradually and rightfully being recognised as an artform. To me, a charged object like the kantha subverts the skewed narrative of textiles as merely a

▲ *Jomi 1* (2021), unpicked vintage quilt, 120 × 90cm (47 × 35in).

decorative medium. Such quotidian objects are a tangible embodiment of a cultural legacy, a definitive anthropological marker tracing the lives of generations of its makers and menders. I hope that increased interest and research in traditions like kantha will foster a deeper understanding of the artform and its community.

I hope that through acquainting ourselves with objects like the kantha and its histories, we celebrate cultural differences more and challenge preconceived notions about craft, its connotations and its practitioners. Even though things have improved within the past few years, the artificial divide between art and craft needs to disappear altogether.

sayanchanda.com

Stitching Stories: Kantha as Self-expression

Women embroidered kantha to express themselves through the medium of stitches. Kantha became a canvas for expressing their world view. The women made intentional choices in the imagery they elected to embroider – either inspired by direct observation, or more abstract ideas – as well as in the threads and stitches they selected to best express their ideas. To me, self-expression is a central tenet of kantha which defines it as an artform although, until recently, this aspect has often been overlooked by art historians and curators. I hope that by recognising kantha as the artform it is, we open ourselves to the power of stitches for narrating our stories.

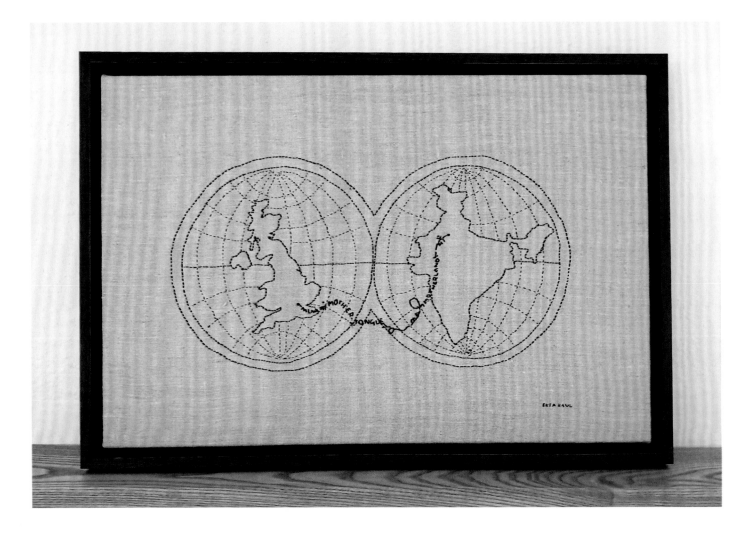

▼ Ekta Kaul, *Hiraeth* (2023) (56 × 38cm [22 × 15in]), explores my longing for a home that no longer exists.

▶ Shezad Dawood
(born London,
England, 1974).

Interview № 7
Shezad Dawood

Shezad Dawood is a multidisciplinary artist who interweaves stories, realities and symbolism to create richly layered artworks, spanning painting, textiles, sculpture, film and digital media. He exhibits internationally and has had his work included in key collections at The Guggenheim, New York; Arts Council Collection, London; Tate, UK; Kiran Nadar Museum of Art, Delhi; Sharjah Art Foundation, UAE; National Gallery of Canada, Ottawa; and The British Museum, London, among others.

EK: Can you share some details about your personal background and how your interest in kantha developed over time?
SD: Although I was born in London, I had strong family connections to both Karachi and Goa, and lived in Karachi between the ages of six and eight. My family had been involved with textiles for quite a few generations, so although it was a bit of a perceived break when I went to art school, there was something quite natural about returning to textiles as a form and base for my work.

The idea of the stitch – and a countervailing stitch – as well as the layers and ridges that would often be built up in kantha and ralli quilts (traditional quilts with applique and patchwork, handmade by women artisans in Sindh, Pakistan and Western India), became a natural correspondence to modernist European ideas of bricolage, and even a non-Western alternative lineage of the 'ready-made'. At art school I already had a stack of textiles I had collected under my bed, as I was unconsciously working out how to incorporate them into my practice.

EK: What themes do you explore in your practice?
SD: I have a lot of respect for craft traditions, although this has changed quite radically since I felt they were undervalued in the contemporary art space when I was starting as an artist. So I began slowly thinking about cutting, stitching, reassembling, printing and painting over the textiles I had. Over time, this has become a complex process of spatial arrangement, and I often spend as long – if not longer – cutting, stitching and reassembling as I do painting on the surface. I think the composition

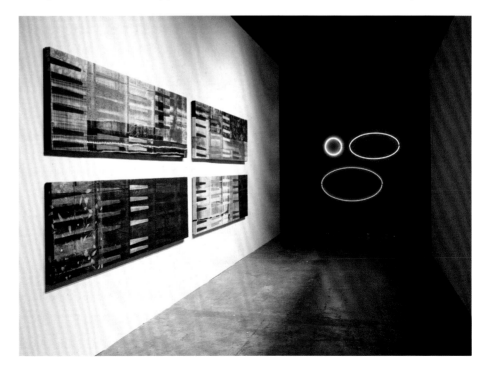

▶ Installation at *Imagined Nations / Modern Utopias* (exhibition at Gwangju Biennale), 2018. Courtesy of the artist and Gwangju Biennale.

▲ *Solid and Voids* (2020), acrylic on vintage textile, 194 × 154cm (76 × 61in).

of different textile elements reflects something fundamental about the process of rearranging the world, and I am quite obsessed about the physicality or sculptural quality of creating something that eventually sits between textile, painting and sculptural relief.

I like to think of continuing a conversation with the original makers of the textiles I work with, and I spent a long time learning how to mimic different stitches so I could then vary them, or play with arranging one textile fragment against another so the stitches are continuous but the pattern is not. All this before adding additional layers of story and meaning via screenprinting, block

printing or painting on the surface. I am interested in a variety of themes, from architecture to cinema, gardens and ecology – since all point to a way of spatialising and narrating the world around us.

EK: Your practice is so wide ranging. Where can we see your work?
SD: My work is in a number of key museum collections such as The Guggenheim, New York; Tate, UK; Kiran Nadar Museum of Art, Delhi; Sharjah Art Foundation, UAE; and the National Gallery of Canada, Ottawa, but it is equally at home in domestic or public settings. For Frieze London LIVE in 2019, I collaborated with

fashion designer Priya Ahluwalia on costumes for dancers, incorporating textile fragments from the studio.

I also work with film, and often collaborate with musicians so there is a constant experimentation that seeks to expand the range of the practice. I see cutting and editing in film as a direct correspondence to cutting and reassembling in textiles.

EK: What does kantha mean to you?
SD: To me, kantha is a continuous dialogue between makers and artists, that at its highest level reaches a symphonic potential where it starts to point to an almost spiritual dimension. I often combine kantha with ceramics, neon and other lighting. I use ceramics to extend this idea of the hand into a vertical object that brings out the physicality in kantha. And I juxtapose kantha works specifically with neon elements to tease out colour and pattern through the use of line, and point it towards a spiritual endpoint by amplifying the perceptual field of both the neon and the kantha in relation to each other.

EK: Which particular aspects of kantha do you find inspiring and how are you exploring it within your work?
SD: I see the use of running stitches as

▲ *Circulation* (2020), 150 × 172cm (59 × 67.7in); *Overhangs* (2020), 215 × 150cm (84.6 × 59in); *Situated Architecture* (2020), 197 × 188cm (77.5 × 74in), all acrylic on vintage textile.

a form of quiet narration that allows me to intervene and reinvent the medium. The other aspect is what I call 'scar tissue', where a particular ridge line leaves a physical vestige of making that is essentially human in the way it references the body.

EK: What is the future of kantha, according to you?
SD: I think it is a living form because it is so connected to the body, both in its making and its form. I love it as a form of narrative building, and that is certainly how I use it. But I have also been interested in how several other artists are using it in unexpected and surprising ways, so I think there is a long and interesting future in

I have also been interested in how several other artists are using it in unexpected and surprising ways, so I think there is a long and interesting future in the medium.

the medium, particularly where it interfaces with other media.

EK: What are your hopes for the future?
SD: I would love to keep developing how I work with textiles – I have made some experiments with hybridising film and textiles that I would like to develop further and more ambitiously. I am currently working on a project looking at ideas of the garden as both a metaphysical and community space, which will build on the work I did with *University of Non-Dualism*, so watch this space for how that evolves.

shezaddawood.com

147

Interview № 8
Bhasha Chakrabarti

Bhasha Chakrabarti has an MFA in painting and printmaking from the Yale School of Art. She has exhibited in solo and group shows at Jeffery Deitch, New York and Los Angeles; Hales, New York; Experimenter, Kolkata; M+B, Los Angeles; Museum of Art and Photography, Bangalore; and Lyles & King, New York.

Chakrabarti is the recipient of the South Asia Artist Prize (SAAI) awarded by the University of California, Berkeley. She was awarded a Beinecke Research Fellowship in 2021 and the Fountainhead Residency in 2020. Bhasha Chakrabarti currently lives and works in New Haven, Connecticut.

EK: Can you share some textile memories from your childhood and how you first encountered kantha?

BC: Growing up in various places around the world, including Hawaii, New York, Kolkata and New Haven, I came to realise a common thread of deep-rooted quilting tradition in all these places. I was fortunate to be surrounded by a variety of quilting styles, including kapa kuiki and flag

▼ *Karvat (The Turn)* (2020), oil on used sari, used clothing, thread, 2.4 × 1.5m (94 × 60in).

◀ Bhasha Chakrabarti (born Honolulu, Hawaii, 1991) in her studio.

▶ *Ma & Me* (2020), ink, acrylic, used clothing, thread, 2.3 × 1.7m (92 × 66in). A self-portrait with my mother in my shadow. As in *Karvat*, I have created this surface using used clothing that belongs to me and my mother. This work was a semi-finalist in the 2022 Outwin Boochever Portrait Competition at the National Portrait Gallery in the Smithsonian.

quilts from Hawaii; Kawandi quilting from Siddi communities in India and Pakistan; Gee's Bend quilts by African-American women in Alabama; and kantha quilting from Bengal.

Being close to kantha is one of my earliest sensory memories. My great-aunt in Kolkata sewed a kantha quilt for me when I was born, using old, soft white saris with red borders. I was swaddled in it as an infant and carried it with me everywhere as a toddler until it fell apart completely.

EK: What is your work about?
BC: My work explores the complexity of cloth as it simultaneously covers and reveals the body. I use textiles in various forms to symbolise human entanglements and histories of oppression and liberation. By centring cloth in my work, I aim to highlight the importance of embodied touch and the potential for mending, patching and quilting together in new ways.

I also challenge Western art histories by embracing excess nudity and eroticism, and leaning into the richness of non-Western textile traditions – to me, it is a way of resisting colonial and capitalist systems. Ultimately, my art making is an excavation of pre-existing historical intimacies, a recognition of interdependencies between marginalised communities, and an imagining of solidarities and alternative futures.

EK: In what settings do you envision your work being displayed?
BC: I deliberately try to make objects – quilts especially – for multiple contexts and spaces. On the one hand, my profession is that of a fine artist, so a lot of my work is destined for galleries and museums. But I also regularly make quilts and objects for friends and family. My cousin had a baby recently, and I sewed a kantha for her, which now occupies her crib.

I am also excited when works that I had made are shown in a gallery context, hung up on the wall, but then are used in a domestic context, as a quilt on the bed, by whoever collects them. This ability for quilts and cloth to bridge so many spaces is crucial to me.

EK: Tell me about the materials and processes you use in your work.
BC: My practice places equal importance on the visual content of painting and the materiality of the cloth on which I paint. I often use kantha as a part of a portrait of a close friend or family member. In those works, I always start by collecting used clothing of the person(s) I intend to make the portrait of. I then layer and sew together those clothing items into a quilt by hand.

I gravitate towards making my quilts out of used clothing, both out of a desire to preserve the element of thrift, which I believe is at the heart of kantha, but also because that allows my work to be both a material and a pictorial embodiment of the person I am painting. I love that items of clothing that have spent countless hours rubbing against the skin of a person are now functioning as a support to a painted depiction of that same person's skin.

◀ *Disco* (2018–22), 2.4 × 2.1m (94½ × 82in). Made in collaboration with Anuradha Dalmiya and Rashmi Varma. This is a part of a series of quilts made using fabric scraps and cuttings from Delhi-based fashion designer Rashmi Varma's studio.

Sometimes, I proceed to wear down the top surfaces of these quilts using sandpaper, in order to expose the fabrics in the in-between or hidden layers, resulting in both a painterly blending effect and a gesture towards the layered process of kantha quilting. Then I make a painting, usually with oil paints, of the subject on this palimpsestic surface composed of their clothing. Often the work is double-sided, in the same way that a functional kantha quilt is meant to be touched on both sides.

EK: How has kantha influenced your work?
BC: Kantha embodies ambiguity and 'in-betweenness' in my practice. The process of hand-quilting – traditionally a domestic activity in Bengal and Bangladesh – takes on a different meaning when collectively re-enacted by women from diverse backgrounds in a modern studio.

This physical intimacy creates a momentary and fragile 'being with the other' that transcends social hierarchies. While primarily functional objects meant to be touched and handled, my kantha also become art when hung on the wall in a gallery setting, oscillating between public and private worlds. This self-reflective and disconcerting

Hand-quilting – traditionally a domestic activity in Bengal and Bangladesh – takes on a different meaning when collectively re-enacted by women from diverse backgrounds in a modern studio.

quality challenges viewers to interpret them from a distance.

EK: I am curious to hear about your work *Karvat (The Turn)*.
BC: In *Karvat*, I have used kantha quilting that I learnt from my mother to create a painted portrait of her as a reclining odalisque. The quilt is made from my grandmother's, mother's and my own used clothing, which have been patched, painted, layered and sewn together. The distressed surface reveals generational sedimentation within the work.

The title refers to the double-sided nature of the quilt and the many transformations happening within it, for instance a functional object intended to cover the body has become an artwork on which the body is being exposed.

bhashachakrabarti.com

▶ Pooja Jagadeesh
(born Mysore
(Karnataka),
India, 1977).

Interview № 9
Pooja Jagadeesh

EK: Tell me a little bit about your childhood or background/ training and how you first became interested in textiles, in particular kantha.

PJ: For as long as I can remember, I have been fascinated by textiles and how people use them, be it as garments or in their homes. My mother's collection of saris definitely played a huge role in shaping my own textile sensibilities, which was further fuelled by growing up around women who shared a passion for the six yards. Living in the hot, tropical climate of Southern India meant being partial to cottons, and the ones from Kolkata and Dhaka were especially coveted for their airy fabrics as well their distinct aesthetics. The ones with kantha embroidery held an extra-special place.

My first exposure to kantha was by way of one such sari that had found its way into my mother's collection. One of the first saris that I ever bought myself as a young working professional right out of design school was a tussar silk kantha. Many years later, coming full circle, I even swaddled my newborn daughter in kantha that my Bengali sister-in-law hand quilted and embroidered especially for her, using my mother's old, softened cotton saris!

While initially the fascination was mostly visual, it was only during my undergraduate studies at the National Institute of Design, Ahmedabad, that I found my interest in the craft of textiles. I majored in graphic design, pursued a long career in branding and have no actual training in textile design, but am truly grateful for the multidisciplinary exposure and approach to design that the institute fostered during those formative years.

EK: What does kantha mean to you?
PJ: In spite of having evolved from a very functional need to upcycle and reuse textiles, I have always thought of kantha more as an art than a craft. The freestyle embroidery has such a strong individualistic approach to pattern-making, where every single stitch has an imprint of the maker. Also, as a textile craft, it has one of the strongest storytelling vocabularies, for example, some of the *nakshi* kantha to me are reminiscent of illustrated picture books! There is something deeply empowering about a craft that allowed women, even if in a marginalised capacity, to express themselves artistically.

▲ Monochrome tussar silk kantha worn by Pooja, and detail of the embroidery.

◀ (*Top*) The embroidery shows a profusion of flora and fauna.
(*Bottom*) Pooja wears her forest-themed *nakshi* kantha sari here. It is interesting to note Pooja's playful drape, which does not include the traditional pleats in the front allowing the pattern to be read as one continuous length. The sari length is also shorter, finishing around the ankles, which adds a contemporary twist.

seamlessly with my lifestyle as well as my existing wardrobe. For that I had to look beyond conventions and my own conditioning to transition from the sari being a traditional, ceremonial garment that I'd only drape for special occasions with a whole lot of help – basically something that seemed very cumbersome – to attire I'd throw on instinctively on any regular day.

It took many small yet incremental steps to deconstruct the sari and reimagine it in ways that I was comfortable with personally. Expanding the definition of what qualifies as a sari blouse, making simple structural changes to the pleats and *pallu* of the conventional Nivi drape, borrowing elements from other vernacular drapes, examining the need for a traditional underskirt or even just the choice of footwear and accessories that are typically associated with saris were some of the things that helped me on my journey.

It's been heartening to see an increasing tribe of people, beyond the constructs of age and gender, who are finding new and exciting ways to make the sari their own. And that's only testament to the versatility of the sari. After all, it's the most inclusive, sustainable, one-size-fits-all garment with an increasing relevance in today's world!

EK: Fewer urban Indian women are choosing to wear the sari as everyday clothing, compared to a generation ago. However, you have embraced the sari and have given it your own flavour in the way you drape and style it, inviting younger women to be more experimental with their saris. Tell me more about your journey with the sari.
PJ: It was not something I set out to do consciously. And looking back, it was a classic case of form following function. Having embraced the sari much later in life, I needed to make it work for me, which then meant finding hacks that could dovetail

EK: On your social media platform, you champion the traditional sari weavers, the embroiderers, as well as contemporary emerging designers who are breaking the mould. You also share the provenance of the pieces you wear. Why does sharing these stories feel important to you and what impact have you noticed?

PJ: At a time when our world is reeling adversely under the impact of fast fashion, local, sustainable and slow may perhaps be the only viable way forward for all humanity. There is no walking that path as Indians without reclaiming our staggering handloom legacy and truly embracing handmade in our everyday and, more importantly, by supporting the sizeable artisan ecosystem that creates them and the industry they continue to depend on for their

At a time when our world is reeling adversely under the impact of fast fashion, local, sustainable and slow may perhaps be the only viable way forward for all humanity.

livelihoods. The handloom sector is still the second-largest employer in our country after agriculture!

As consumers it is imperative to understand how our purchasing power can influence the very nature of products themselves and, in turn, how that can impact the environment and entire economies. One does not have to be an expert, but educating ourselves about a craft and its provenance, and championing pathbreaking designers and meaningful design interventions will only help us make better choices.

EK: Tell me about your kantha saris. What drew you to them? Are there any stories about them that you'd like to share?

PJ: I don't own many, but the few kantha that I do – not just saris but also stoles and dupattas –were collected over decades from various sources. Like I already mentioned, the first sari I ever bought myself was a monochromatic tussar silk kantha. As a young professional who wanted to be taken seriously, I loved that it made me look much older than my age. It is more than two decades old now and everything about it – the design, the fabric, the embroidery – has aged beautifully. I drape it more often now than I ever did back then and in far more interesting ways!

My favourite, though, is a whimsical forest-themed *nakshi* kantha sari, bought when I knew a lot more about the craft and was more mindful of who made my clothes. I was told it took artisan Rekha Mondal in Santiniketan more than five months to embroider it.

EK: What is the future of kantha according to you?

PJ: I'm quite optimistic about the future of crafts, including kantha. Even as we debate how pervasive AI will come to be in the near future, there is an evident shift globally towards artisanal luxury and a renewed enthusiasm in the design community to preserve hand skills and reimagine our traditional crafts for the new world. For a craft like kantha, where the human aspect is integral to its very existence, it could translate into being an exciting medium, not just for creating functional products but also art.

Unlike weaving or other highly technical and skilled forms of embroidery, the building block of a kantha is nothing but a simple running stitch, out of which could evolve a more contemporary vocabulary for the craft that makers of today could use to tell their stories.

instagram.com/poojajagadeesh

Kantha as a Journal

Motifs reflecting everyday life, current events and memories grace the kantha. Kantha serves as a visual and tactile journal of the artist's life; their interests, opinions and dreams. Kantha invites us to be more present by documenting and reflecting on the daily rituals, simple objects or ephemera that forms the background fabric of our lives. I map my daily walks using narrative stitch, as below.

◀ Ekta Kaul, *Meditative Walk* (2022), 90 × 90cm (35.4 × 35.4in).

▷ Lynn Setterington (born Doncaster, Yorkshire, 1960) in her studio.

Interview № 10
Lynn Setterington

Lynn Setterington is a British textile artist. Her work explores contemporary issues in society and how stitch can be used to commemorate people and communities. Her quilts and cloths are held in museum collections including the Victoria & Albert Museum, London; Denver Art Museum, Colorado; Crafts Council, London; and Whitworth Art Gallery, Manchester. Setterington cites a visit to the *Woven Air* exhibition that showcased kantha quilts from Bangladesh and Bengal at the Whitechapel Gallery, London, in the late 1980s as a significant influence on her work.

EK: What sparked your initial fascination with stitch and, more specifically, kantha?
LS: I developed an interest in embroidery during my primary school years, which eventually led me to pursue an arts degree in embroidery at Goldsmiths College in London. In 1987, I was introduced to kantha when I visited the *Woven Air* exhibition at the Whitechapel Gallery. The exhibition highlighted the use of stitch to portray everyday domestic objects, which I loved.

The fact that kantha quilts were made entirely from recycled materials was a huge draw for me. The impact

of the exhibition was so profound that it altered the course of my work, and I became captivated by kantha. This fascination eventually took me to Bangladesh, where I collaborated with numerous women's embroidery groups. I have continued to work with women's groups in the UK and Bangladesh since the early 1990s.

EK: What specific elements of kantha inspire you, and in what ways are you incorporating them into your creative process?
LS: I am inspired by a variety of

▽ *Home Alone* (1994), 70 × 90cm (27½ × 35½in).

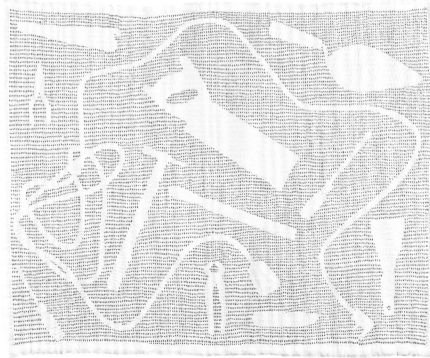

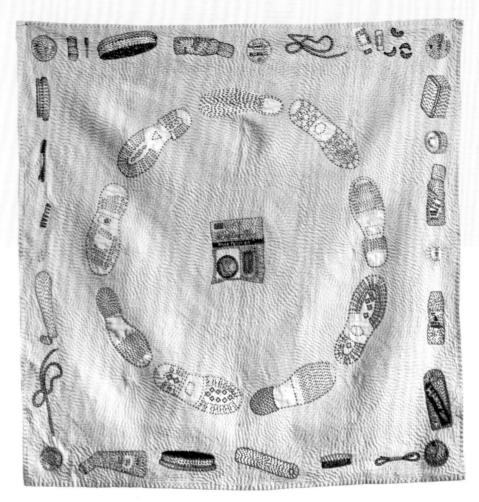

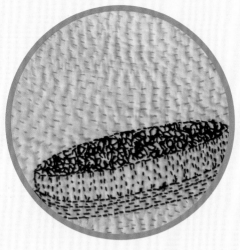

◁ *Shoe Shine* (1996), 1.2 × 1.1m (47 × 43in).

stitch overlooked everyday rituals. It pays homage to a local shoe repair shop, now sadly closed, where shoes could be re-soled or mended, and laces and shoe polish in all colours were for sale. It is also a tribute to my dad, who liked to shine his leather shoes before work, which I remember as a child.

I used a circular stitch motif for the background of this quilt. In each of my kantha embroideries, I adapt different background stitch patterns.

EK: In your opinion, what lies ahead for kantha?
LS: Kantha has been studied widely and embraced globally. As the tradition evolves and adapts to modern times, it continues to remain pertinent and thrive. My hope is that kantha stitching remains a slow and meaningful act, fostering a sense of unity and dialogue among people.

EK: What advice do you have for someone just starting their kantha journey?
LS: Take time and enjoy working with your hands. Make sure you test colour combinations and explore different threads.

lynnsetterington.co.uk

elements in kantha. The masterful embroidery techniques used in early kantha, as well as their storytelling qualities, have always inspired me. Additionally, the repurposing of materials, nods to folk art, rural life and everyday experiences are all aspects of kantha that I deeply appreciate. I'm drawn to the simplicity of kantha, and the fact that it is traditionally practised by women adds to its unique cultural significance. In my own creative process, I strive to incorporate these elements in new and interesting ways, experimenting with different materials, techniques and designs to create unique works that pay homage to the rich tradition of kantha.

EK: Tell me about some of your kantha projects where you have drawn inspiration from everyday objects that are sometimes overlooked.
LS: My piece *Home Alone* (1994) documents my move from London to Manchester and so captures a moment in time, including the purchase of my first house and my first adventure living on my own in a new city.

The imagery moves away from predominantly floral motifs found in historic kantha quilts and instead depicts a series of everyday objects, tools and DIY items normally associated with male hobbies and preoccupations. I also began exploring etching around that time, so the black-and-white colour scheme and vertical stitched marks were driven by this new approach.

Shoe Shine (1996) captures details from ordinary life and celebrates in

The Poetics of Damage

The weathered patination of copper, crumbling layers of paint, torn shreds of posters on urban walls, graphic cracks in the pavement, soft colours of wilting magnolias and tattered layers of kantha all speak of a beauty that I call 'the poetics of damage'. I have always felt drawn to it and began exploring ageing as inspiration for art-making, during my master's degree.

To me, the worn-out kantha surface is so beautiful. I love how it tells stories of holding bodies, rich histories and lived experiences that are woven into its very fabric. The holes and tears reveal the hidden strata of the fabric, hinting at the lives the cloth has lived before being repurposed into the quilt, and invites us to imagine stories of homes and people the kantha became a part of. Excavating the sediments of kantha reveals stories of care, repair and beauty to be found in the tatters.

▼ Mending and caring for older kantha went hand in hand with creating new pieces. Collection of the National Crafts Museum, New Delhi.

Interview № 11
Katie Mawson

Katie Mawson trained as a textile designer and has run a successful knitwear business for many years. More recently, she has moved into fine art. Katie celebrates the beauty to be found in the faded and the tattered; she uses the cloth from vintage books as both her palette and canvas. Using an array of colours – many of them faded and marked through time, attesting to their former life – Katie fashions the discarded book cloths into arresting artworks.

EK: Tell me a little bit about how you first became interested in textiles.
KM: I developed an interest in knitting and spinning at a young age. I was around ten when I learnt to knit, and by the age of thirteen I had picked up spinning using a spindle. At fifteen I became skilled enough to use a spinning wheel.

My fascination with kantha began during a trip to Rajasthan, India in the early 1990s. I remember visiting a village where I came across some stunning bedspreads using simple running stitches. The people there were incredibly welcoming, and the kantha work was simply exquisite – colourful and masterfully crafted. I was deeply moved by this experience, and it left a profound impact on me.

The running stitch has become an important element for me in my art.

EK: What themes do you explore within your practice?
KM: I work with vintage book cloth from discarded books. I have a huge love of colour and texture; with this medium the two meet perfectly. I am inspired by my local landscape, particularly Ullswater, and also I love the beauty in dereliction and abandoned old buildings.

▼ *Groynes One* (2020), 22 × 29cm (8.6 × 11.4in).

EK: Which particular aspects of kantha do you find inspiring and how are you exploring them within your work?
KM: To me, kantha is a slow, methodical way of absorbing myself in a creative flow of stitch and line. I love the repetition of creating the stitches. There is a catharsis – in my own work I use it mostly to create textural blocks of colour and shape.

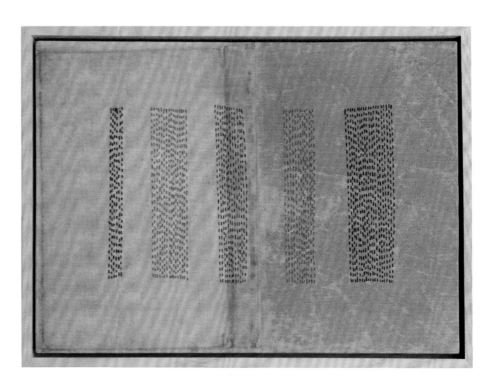

◀ Katie Mawson
(born Cumbria, 1963)
in her studio.

▶ *Stranded* (2020),
44 × 38cm (17 × 15in).

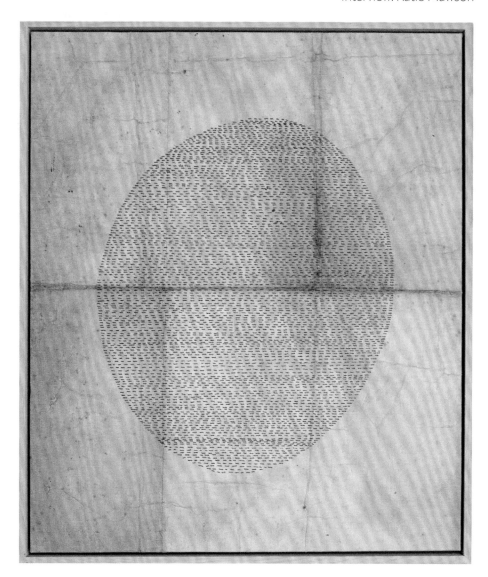

EK: We have talked about our mutual love of weathering and the decay process as inspiration on previous occasions. Where else do you draw inspiration from?
KM: I live in the Lake District and swim at sunrise at my local lake throughout the year; the quiet and calm of these swims – along with the changes in weather and seasons – inform my work, as does the ageing process within more urban environments. I like to juxtapose the beauty of urban decay and dereliction with the purity of nature.

EK: What materials and processes do you use in your work?
KM: I slice, cut, rip and skin marked and faded cloths from boards that bind books. I deconstruct them and reconstruct them into something new. I often spend hours arranging and rearranging shapes and colours, starting with one idea that evolves into something else along the way. I like this fluidity; for me it is all about colour balance, positive and negative spaces and creating a sense of tranquillity.

To me, kantha is a slow, methodical way of absorbing myself in a creative flow of stitch and line.

EK: What is the future of kantha according to you?
KM: As with all ancient crafts, we need to encourage the younger generation to become involved in hands-on creation. I think it is really important to keep these textile traditions going and pass them on down the generations – much harder today than it was in the past due to the fast digital pace we live in.

EK: What advice would you give to someone who is just starting their journey into kantha?
KM: Give in to the slow pace and enjoy it. Wax your thread to help prevent tangles!

katiemawsonart.com

159

A Symphony of Marks

To me, kantha stitches have the ability to lend themself to abstract mark making. We can create interesting textures and graphic marks on the cloth by incorporating rhythm – an important principle of art – in the work. Dynamic linear rhythms can be created through simple repetition and variation to create movement and energy in the composition, while breaking the monotony of a repeating pattern.

In my work *Fields of Serenity*, I have used repetition of marks and variations in the stitch size, weight of thread and stitch placement to create rhythms and interest in the composition.

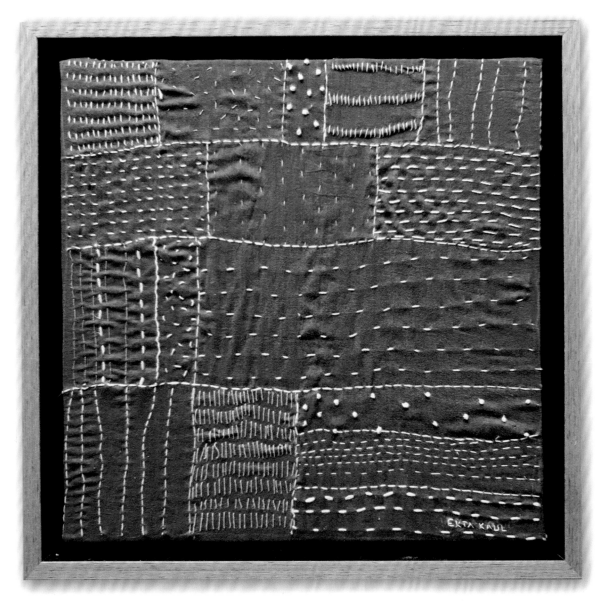

◄ Ekta Kaul, *Fields of Serenity* (2023), 23 × 30cm (11.4 × 11.8in). Tatter Blue Library collection.

Interview № 12
Swati Kalsi

▶ Swati Kalsi (born Delhi, India, 1981).

Delhi-based, award-winning designer Swati Kalsi works from her atelier, which overlooks an ancient Mughal monument, a tranquil place in the busy South Delhi design district of Hauz Khas village.

Swati's sophisticated designs are expertly crafted with intricate graphic patterns using stitches inspired by sujani – an embroidery tradition from Bihar that is closely related to kantha in its ethos of using repurposed discarded cloth and the use of running stitch embroidery.

As Bihar and Bengal are neighbouring states in East India, their geographical proximity has led to rich cultural exchanges over centuries, evident in the similarities in the kantha and sujani traditions. Ranging from one-of-a-kind pieces to small editions, Swati's textiles have been welcomed into exhibitions, galleries, homes of international collectors and museums such as the Victoria & Albert Museum, where they were featured as part of the *Fabric of India* exhibition. They are a testament to the beauty of traditional techniques, skilfully reimagined for the modern world.

▲ *SHE LL* (2015), 5 × 3m (16 × 10ft).

EK: Tell me about your background.
SK: My parents were early creative influences and encouraged me to explore the arts. As a child I remember being interested in fine arts and performing arts, eventually honing in on fashion in my teens. I pursued this and studied fashion at India's National Institute of Fashion Technology (NIFT) and later at the Domus Academy, Milan for a master's degree.

EK: How and when were you introduced to traditional Indian embroidery traditions like sujani?
SK: Early on in my career, I participated in a World Bank initiative, where I had the opportunity to collaborate closely with sujani artisans in rural Bihar and banjara embroidery artisans in Andhra Pradesh. Through my involvement in the project, I not only gained a deeper understanding of craft traditions at the grassroots, but also developed a love of stitch. This experience eventually led me to establish my atelier in 2012, with the aim of empowering the rural women artisans through creative collaborations and bringing a contemporary aesthetic to the time-honoured Indian handcrafted textiles, with a particular emphasis on sujani embroidery.

EK: Where do you draw your inspiration from?
SK: My biggest source of inspiration

is nature. I have always felt drawn to gradations and rhythms in nature. I also find traditional Indian embroidery techniques, especially the sujani tradition, deeply inspiring. Sujani is a poetic embroidery style that is also highly functional, binding ingenuity and frugality in a beautiful way. The intricate surface created by the interplay of simple running stitches, with their varying intensities, sizes and colours, suggests the layered depths and rhythms of nature. Over time, this has become my vocabulary, with the emerging layers and diluting depths providing a rich texture that fuels my creative process. To me, sujani stitches reflect the spirit of their creator, providing a unique lens through which to explore the endless possibilities of texture and pattern.

EK: Tell me about your materials and processes.
SK: I work with natural fabrics, such as silks, cottons and linens, that I develop in collaboration with master weavers in different parts of India. I collaborate with a small group of women artisans through interactive creative workshops and we cocreate the pieces together. I believe the human hand has an intuitive intelligence of its own, far beyond what our rational minds or machines are capable of. It is that spirit I seek

▶ *Style 5* (work in progress) (2013), Collection Minor.

▶ *Flying Windows* (2012), Collection Anhad.

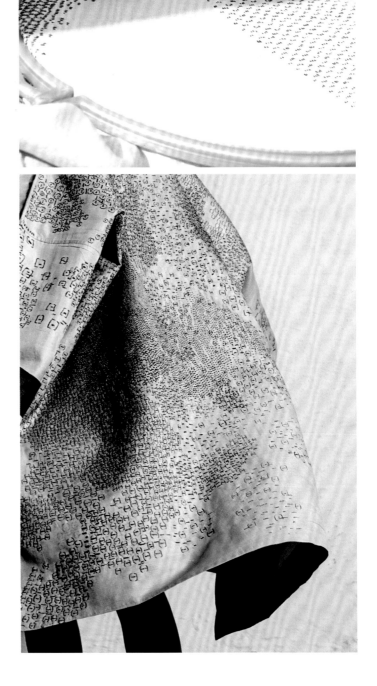

▲ *Style 3* (2013), Collection Minor.

▲ *Style 6* (2012), Collection Anhad.

to harness through my embroideries. Innovation, hand-craftsmanship and addressing social issues through creativity are central to my work.

EK: Can you describe how you translate your love of patterns in nature into embroidery?
SK: *Anhad* (meaning 'boundless' in Hindi) is a clothing range I created in collaboration with sujani artisans from Muzaffarpur district, Bihar. The collection was inspired by my love of naturally occurring patterns, particularly fractals, which are patterns formed from chaotic equations that contain self-similar patterns of complexity that increase with magnification. They can be found in various natural phenomena, such as rivers, blood vessels, DNA and clouds, and follow a deterministic pattern, despite their unpredictable nature.

In Anhad, the embroidery patterns were allowed to grow organically, much like fractals, following an instinctive rhythm.

In Anhad, the embroidery patterns were allowed to grow organically, much like fractals, following an instinctive rhythm. The resulting self-similar patterns of embroidery spread abstractly over the surface of the garments, creating a unique surface.

EK: I remember seeing your work 'SHE LL'. It is beautiful. Can you tell me more about it?
'SHE LL' was commissioned as part of *Fracture: Indian Textiles, New Conversations*, an exhibition

of contemporary textiles by Devi Art Foundation in Delhi. The work seeks to portray the protective and nurturing role of women through the metaphor of an embroidered shawl.

I drew inspiration from sujani, which serves multiple functions rooted in ancient beliefs. Cloth bound together by sujani stitches was used ritually to invoke the presence of Chitriya Ma, the deity of the tatters, and to express the Indian belief that all parts belong to the whole and must return to it.

Traditionally, sujani was also used to wrap newborns. The term 'sujani' reflects this functional nature, with 'su' meaning easy and facilitating, and 'jani' meaning birth. Thus a sujani embroidered shawl became the perfect vehicle to express ideas of love, care and protection.

swatikalsi.com

163

Kantha as Empowerment

Although the domestic practice of embroidering kantha has continued in an unbroken continuum, kantha making became institutionalised in several waves. As Pika Ghosh notes in *Making Home, Making Kantha*, in 1905 kantha began to be collected and exhibited by nationalist thinkers and leaders creating a unified Bengali identity. This was an effort to challenge the first partition of Bengal implemented by the British colonial administration, which had resulted in separating the largely Muslim eastern areas from the largely Hindu western areas. Kantha was positioned as a wholesome, quintessentially Bengali activity, practised by Bengali women regardless of their religion. Women's groups were set up to teach the kantha in and around Santiniketan. Gurusaday Dutt, an Indian civil servant, built up an extensive collection of kantha between 1929 and 1939, which later became Gurusaday

Museum on the outskirts on Kolkata. Sadly, I could not see the collections in person as the Gurusaday museum has been closed for the last several years.

Institutionalised kantha making gained further momentum in the 1950s in response to the need for creating livelihoods for women in the newly independent India, especially those who were uprooted from their ancestral homes and lands as a result of the partition of Bengal and had to move across borders to West Bengal from East Bengal (present-day Bangladesh) or vice versa, leaving their homes and possessions behind.

Several institutions, including NGOs, entrepreneurs and designers, led this movement to enable the Bengali women to create an income through kantha making so that they could support their families. Typically,

◀ Kantha scarf embroidered by members of the Street Survivors India using two layers of vintage saris, 2023.

fabrics, threads and designs were provided to the women, who embroidered kantha at home and brought the finished items to a central collection point or had their kantha collected by institution representatives from their homes. The women were able to work from home and received payments for their embroidery.

From here, the kantha were sent off to shops or emporia, or sold at craft fairs in metropolitan cities of India, like Delhi, Mumbai and Kolkata, as well as those abroad. Slowly, over the years, fashion, accessories and homeware products, such as saris, scarves, stoles and tunics, began to be made using kantha stitches as embellishment. The universe of kantha products continues to grow and find global audiences. I interviewed founders and senior members of several organisations such as the fair trade cooperative SASHA, SHE (Self-Help Enterprise) Kantha, Weavers Studio and Crafts Council of West Bengal in Kolkata, all of whom are doing exemplary work in creating opportunities for women to gain economic independence through kantha embroidery, by providing training and fair wages, establishing a market for their kantha, and investing in healthcare and the education of the women and their families. Today, many contemporary Indian designers incorporate kantha embroidery in their collections and work with fair-trade groups to produce them. British homeware brand TOAST works with women groups who are part of SASHA in West Bengal to produce coats and quilts.

Although this way of kantha making is far removed from the more personalised and family-centred, traditional kantha making, it has become a force of empowerment for the women, providing them with economic independence and, in effect, a voice.

▲ Contemporary coin purses with kantha embroidery, from Byloom, Kolkata.

Today, many contemporary Indian designers incorporate kantha embroidery in their collections and work with fair trade groups to produce them.

Interview № 13
Pritikana Goswami

Pritikana Goswami is renowned for her exquisite kantha. Based in Sonarpur on the outskirts of Kolkata, West Bengal, Pritikana has been making kantha for over thirty years. She was recently awarded one of India's highest civilian awards, the Padma Shri, by the government of India in recognition of her distinguished contribution to kantha.

Entirely self-taught, Pritikana not only supported her family with her kantha making over the years, but also trained hundreds of women in kantha skills, so they could support their own families and keep the kantha tradition alive. As commercial kantha making became more popular, she was dismayed at the decline in the quality that profit margins often dictated.

Determined to keep practising the highest level of craftsmanship, in 2015 the mother-daughter duo, Pritikana Goswami and Mahua Lahiri, together with Mahua's college friend and business partner Suparna Sen, created Hushnohana, a studio and workshop devoted to pursuing museum-quality kantha and reviving traditional designs. Today, the studio employs a small team of local women, who they have trained over several years, and creates kantha wall art, homewares and garments.

▲ Mayur Pankhi Nouko, 48 × 43cm (19 × 17in), embroidered by Jaba Das, Hushnohana, Kolkata..

◀ Pritikana Goswami (born Uluberia, India, 1959) with the other two Hushnohana founders, Mahua Lahiri and Suparna Sen.

▶ Pader (Parer) kantha, 76 × 71cm (30 × 28in) embroidered by Soma Maity, Hushnohana, Kolkata.

EK: How did your journey into kantha begin?

PG: I came to kantha through great personal struggle. In 1973, while I was still in secondary school, I lost my father suddenly. The family income disappeared overnight, so I resolved to support my family through my needlework. I began to take on commissions from acquaintances to embroider saris, and taught myself a wide range of embroidery and mending techniques including kantha, metallic thread and crewel embroidery. Slowly, through word of mouth, I began to get more commissions, but the income remained meagre. Despite this, I never gave up on my needlework. After many years of struggle, a chance meeting with Ruby Palchoudhuri (visionary curator and the then secretary of The Crafts Council of West Bengal) changed the course of my life.

After seeing my embroideries, Ruby asked me to lead and train a group of women in traditional *nakshi* kantha, in an effort to revive the illustrative kantha of the old. Although I was not certain of what this would entail, or even the nuances of *nakshi* kantha, I agreed. Working with a small vintage *nakshi* kantha that Ruby gave me to study, I taught myself kantha stitches.

With Ruby di's help I established a small kantha workshop and training school: we began with nine women. Together, we studied kantha pieces in the Gurusaday Museum and Asutosh Museum archives in Kolkata, and created kantha quilts. My emphasis remained on achieving the highest quality of embroidery, and I inculcated this in my students, too. For instance, I insisted on a smaller stitch size and even rows of stitches, even though they take longer to make. Slowly, our kantha began to find an audience with discerning collectors – not just in India but also in the US and Japan. Over the years, I have trained hundreds of women in kantha and our kantha have graced exhibitions, collectors' homes and museums. I feel so proud of what we have achieved.

EK: What are your favourite tools, materials and processes?

PG: We begin our pieces with a drawing based on a theme in our studio workshop. We do not trace from a template, but draw directly

Rhythm of Charkha (2023), 81 × 81cm (32 × 32in). Designed by Mahua Lahiri, embroidered by Pritikana Goswami, Soma Maity, Pampa Paul, Mahua Pramanik, Sabita Maity, Pampa Debnath, Jaba Das and Mahua Lahiri, for the *Stutr Santati* exhibition.

onto the fabric using a washable pencil. We work with a minimum of two layers, sometimes more: cotton and silk for the top layer and a very fine cotton calico for the lining. In a departure from our usual two layers, we create scarves on a single layer of silk georgette for a Japanese client.

My favourite threads to embroider with are cotton floss; usually I work with two strands. I use needles of varying thickness ranging from nos. 9 to 12, depending on the design. For fine embroidery, I like to use no. 12 needles.

EK: Kantha skills were traditionally passed on from mother to daughter. Your daughter Mahua has joined hands with you and she is taking your legacy forward. Does it feel like life has come full circle?
PG: Yes, I feel so happy that my daughter Mahua is carrying the legacy forward. She grew up observing me embroidering and picked up the stitches simply through tacit learning. Later, she went on to train in design and worked in the fashion industry for several years. However, she was

hesitant to pursue kantha, quite likely because she'd seen my struggles. However, in 2015 she decided to give up her full-time job and together we established Hushnohana – our kantha studio and workshop – along with her friend, Suparna Sen. I could not be more proud.

EK: You described kantha as life-changing. Can you elaborate?
PG: Kantha has transformed my life and the lives of the women I have trained. Through our stitches we have expressed ourselves, we have provided for our families and received respect and recognition in our community and beyond. It is so empowering to be able to do that!

EK: What is the future of kantha according to you?
PG: Kantha is more than a stitch or a textile. It is the embodiment of cultural heritage and the freedom to earn a living with dignity. In my view, it needs to be preserved for future generations.

instagram.com/hushnohana

Creating Your Own Kantha

The vibrant tradition of kantha embroidery presents a treasure trove of creative opportunities to delve into. Within this art form, you will discover the freedom to express yourself and infuse stitches with personal meaning, forge a connection with your interiority and engage in sustainable practices by repurposing discarded cloth. The meditative act of kantha stitching is an invitation to being present in the moment, finding calm amidst the dizzying speed of twenty-first-century living.

Whether you choose to explore a specific strand of kantha, such as storytelling, mindfulness or sustainability, or embrace kantha in its entirety, the key is to allow your kantha to become an embodiment of what interests and moves you – a receptacle for your stories – just as it has always been for the women who have embroidered kantha.

In this chapter we will discuss the elements for creating your own kantha in three broad categories: design, embroidery and display. Whether you are new to kantha embroidery or a seasoned practitioner, this chapter aims to equip you with the necessary tools for creating your kantha and ignite your inspiration, empowering you to embrace this enriching tradition on your own creative path.

◄ The tools and materials which I use when embroidering.

Design Inspiration

Powerful art is deeply personal. Delving into what you find meaningful, moving or beautiful will lead you to authentic, potent art because it will be highly personal and unlike anyone else's. Even if you have never made art, you have an innate ability to choose – for instance, you may feel drawn to a certain shade of blue and intuitively reach for it when you come to buy anything for your home or yourself.

As artist Nicholas Wilton says, this ability to choose between alternatives is your inner artistic voice, and that is what I would like you to tune in to when you come to create your kantha. Do not worry about 'rules', or perfection in stitch techniques, or comparisons with others. The essence of kantha is self-expression, and that is what I would like you to bear in mind.

▼ Observing urban textures on your walks can provide so many exciting ideas for surfaces.

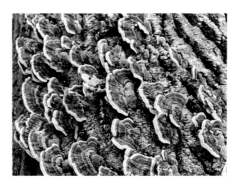

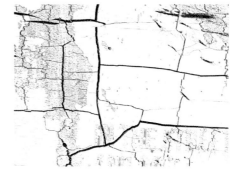

To develop a design for your kantha, take a moment to consider the themes you might want to explore. An effective approach for doing this is to create a personal inspiration list. Begin by brainstorming in your sketchbook and jot down everything you love and feel drawn to, for example vibrant balloons, blooming spring blossoms, captivating urban textures and so on. Be specific and avoid generic terms like 'nature' or 'flowers'; instead, specify the particular ones that captivate you, such as hibiscus, roses or magnolias.

Another source of inspiration is your daily rituals. Consider which activities you find restorative or invigorating, like morning meditation, swimming, enjoying a cup of coffee, nature walks or spending time with your family.

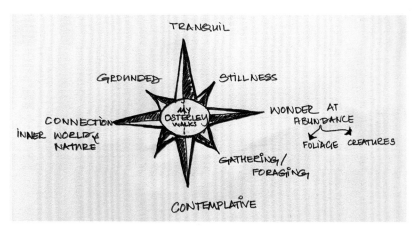

Additionally, delve into your personal experiences and memories. Choosing a subject that holds deep personal significance and reflects who you are as a person will make your kantha unique. From your inspiration list, select a few elements to incorporate into your kantha design, and leave the rest for further exploration and additional design ideas in the future.

▲ Brainstorm a list of anchor words that express the feelings you want to evoke through your art.

Sketching

Before committing to a design, I recommend drawing your ideas in your sketchbook. This practice allows you to visualise your composition and make necessary adjustments. Do not feel precious about your sketchbook; it is simply a tool to record your ideas. Let it be messy and personal.

Begin by creating small thumbnail sketches to test different compositions, focusing on finding a balance between elements. At this stage, your design doesn't need to be finalised as it will evolve as you embroider and quilt. Choose the sketch that excites you the most.

▶ I incorporate drawings of what I encounter on my daily walks to capture in stitch.

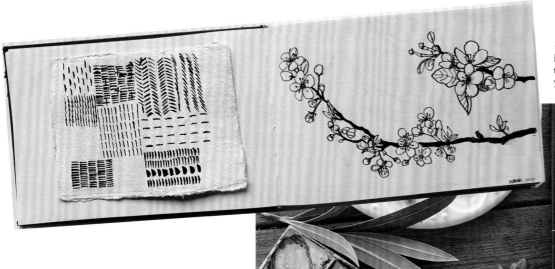

Composition

Composition refers to the arrangement of motifs and shapes within a kantha. It involves how different elements – such as the central lotus, animal and human figures, borders and geometric patterns – are organised and positioned in relation to each other to create a visually pleasing and harmonious overall design.

Classic Composition

If you are drawn to the classic composition of illustrative kantha, you can opt for a central motif as the main focal point, positioning traditional motifs like the Tree of Life, paisleys or others at the corners and borders. As you progress, consider replacing one or more of the classic motifs with elements from your own life or imagination. For example, replace the lotus with your favourite flower, cherished object or visual representation of a special memory. Use your own photography or drawing, refer to images from books or the internet, and use the kantha images in this book as references to develop your own unique motifs.

Non-representational Style

You may want to explore a non-representational style, as seen in abstract kantha, and experiment with geometric shapes, textures and colours to create your composition. This approach encourages you to play with abstract elements to evoke emotions and convey meaning in your kantha design.

The Rule of Thirds

In addition, you can depart from the traditional kantha layout and explore different composition techniques, such as the rule of thirds. This widely used guideline in art and design suggests dividing your embroidery

▲ When sketching, you can use pencils, paints, pens or any medium you like. Take inspiration from what is around you, for example the plants in your garden or on a woodland walk.

You may want to explore a non-representational style, as seen in abstract kantha, and experiment with geometric shapes, textures and colours to create your composition.

▶ Detail of *Meditative Walk* (2022, 90 × 90cm [35.4 ×35.4in]) by Ekta Kaul.

piece into a grid of nine equal parts, using two horizontal and two vertical lines. By placing your main subject or focal point along these lines or at the intersection points, you can achieve a balanced and visually captivating composition. This technique provides a framework for experimentation and enables you to explore different placements, resulting in a dynamic and engaging design.

I encourage you to embrace creativity and trust your intuition when designing your kantha. Whether you choose the classic layout, opt for the rule of thirds or explore other composition techniques, trust your inner voice.

Balanced Composition

A balanced composition is one that invites the viewer's eye to travel around the design in a specific sequence, creating a harmonious feeling. Contrast, balance and harmony are important art principles that must work together to create strong designs. Just as when we eat, we experience strong flavours first and the more subtle flavours come

through slowly afterwards, design the viewer's journey with intention to create balance and harmony in your designs. Include areas of high value contrast, or contrast in scale or textures to invite the viewer to look as soon as they encounter the work, and then create other areas that invite the viewer's eye to rest and linger.

A balanced composition is one that invites the viewer's eye to travel around the design in a specific sequence.

Size

I would suggest starting with a small-sized project, such as 20 × 20cm (8 × 8in) or 25 × 25cm (10 × 10in). Beginning with a smaller size allows you to test your ideas, make refinements and build momentum. Starting with a large project right away can sometimes lead to feelings of overwhelm or frustration. Once you have gained experience and confidence, you can then explore creating kantha on a larger scale. This progression allows you to gradually expand your skills and tackle more ambitious projects at your own pace without becoming overwhelmed.

Transferring Your Design

▲ Kantha exploring
the theme of healing
by Raquel Calado.

Select a design and then draw it to scale
in order to fit it on to your fabric. Scaling
your original drawing up or down can be
done freehand, using a photocopier or by
scanning your drawing and printing in at
the desired size. This process ensures that
your design is proportionate and ready for
transfer onto the fabric.

Once your design drawing is the required
size, it is ready to be transferred onto the
fabric. There are several ways to transfer your

designs (see pages 113–15). I use a combination
of freehand drawing and tracing using heat-
erasable pens to transfer my drawings onto the
fabric surface. The fine tip of the pen allows me
to get intricate details down on the fabric.

Water-soluble pens, chalk and air-drying
pencils are some other options to consider.
Heat-erasable pens work well on a light-
coloured base fabric; however, for darker base
fabrics consider using dressmakers' carbon
paper or light-coloured chalk pens.

Choosing Your Colour Palette

Colour is an important element of your composition, and can dramatically change the feel of your work. Consider the colours you want to use in your design and how they will interact with each other. I use monochrome or colourful palettes based on the overall feeling I am trying to evoke through the work, for example whether I want the work to convey tranquillity, excitement or nostalgia. Use your theme to give you clues for choosing your colour palette; for example, analogous colours (hues that are adjacent to each other on the colour wheel) can be used together to create harmony and evoke soothing emotions.

Laying lengths of threads from the spool or skein onto the fabric can be helpful in selecting colours that interact well with the fabric and the overall colour palette. By visually assessing how the threads interact with the fabric and other colours, you can make informed choices about the colours that best complement your project. This hands-on approach allows you to experiment and find the perfect combination of thread colours that brings your kantha to life.

◀ For *Meditative Walk* (p. 154), I drew inspiration from the soft hues of the landscape at sunrise.

▼ Local flora can offer inspiration for colour and motifs.

▲ Nature is a wonderful resource to go to for inspiration for your colour palette. I suggest photographing colourful botanicals or landscapes that you feel drawn to and then examining the hues. I forage for flowers wherever I travel and use a flower press to flatten and build a reference herbarium.

▶ Unravel a length of each thread and lay them on your fabric to help you decide which ones work well together.

Colour Theory

An understanding of the fundamentals of colour theory will help you make informed choices in selecting colours and ultimately in creating strong compositions. There are three properties of colour:

1   **Hue:** This refers to the name of the colour, for example cadmium red or ochre yellow.

2   **Value:** This refers to how light or dark a colour is. Tints are light values, which are made by mixing white with a colour. Shades are dark values made by mixing black with a colour.

3   **Chroma:** This refers to how saturated or intense the colour is.

Familiarity with colour theory principles, such as complementary or analogous colours, will help you create a harmonious and balanced design.

Selecting Your Fabrics

Fabrics that hold personal meaning for you are the most potent materials to use for creating your kantha. I highly recommend utilising what you have available. Discarded preloved clothing, weathered or ripped fabrics that can no longer be used, old tablecloths or vintage linens are all excellent options to consider.

If you prefer to use new fabrics, I suggest selecting a medium-weight cotton or linen as the top fabric and a fine, lightweight cotton voile, fine muslin or *mulmul* as the lining. You can incorporate additional layers, if desired, but I recommend a minimum of two layers. While there is no strict limit to the number of layers, it's important to consider how easily your

needle can pass through the fabric. Test it out to ensure optimal stitching ease. Additionally, when choosing fabrics, opt for light- to medium-weight options and avoid heavier materials like denim that can be challenging for hand embroidery.

Personally, I love working with linen in my own projects. There are several reasons for this. Firstly, the slubby texture of linen lends a wonderful character to the fabric. Secondly, linen is recognised as one of the most sustainable fibres due to its minimal water requirements for cultivation. Lastly, it is a fabric that is easy to embroider on, offering an enjoyable stitching experience.

Tools
Needles

For Embroidery

For general embroidery work, I recommend using a no. 9 embroidery needle. If you need to add finer details to your design, you can opt for a no. 10 embroidery needle, which offers more precision. Embroidery needles have a sharp tip and can therefore pierce the fabric with ease.

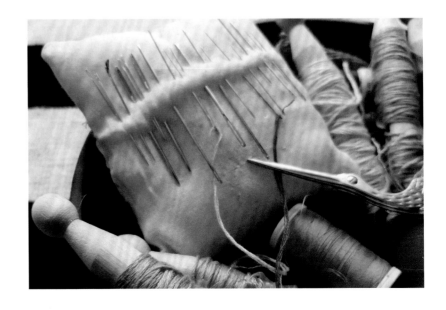

◀ A needle, some thread, and a sharp pair of embroidery scissors are all you'll need to embroider your kantha. I highly recommend using a metal-tipped silicone thimble and needle pullers to protect your fingers.

For Quilting

When it comes to quilting your kantha, I suggest using Milliners needles. These have a sharp tip, are longer than embroidery needles and have a consistent diameter throughout their length, allowing you to pick up multiple stitches at a time and easily pass through several layers of fabric. This makes them well-suited for quilting tasks, providing efficiency and ease of use. Nos. 3, 5 and 7 are good options to consider for size.

For Interlacing Stitches

Tapestry needles are ideal for interlaced stitches because they have a blunt tip, and so when working interlaced stitches it allows you to pass the needle underneath the stitch, without piercing the thread or the fabric.

For Thicker Yarns

Chenille needles have sharp tips and much larger eyes than embroidery needles, although they can be a bit shorter in length. Their larger eyes make them ideal for working with wool or any fancy yarns.

Hoops

The use of a hoop while embroidering and quilting kantha is optional. Traditionally, hoops were not used; however, they have grown in popularity. Personally, I use a hoop for embroidery and choose to quilt my kantha without a hoop as it allows for a more pronounced texture. I encourage you to try it with a hoop and without and decide your preference based on what feels comfortable.

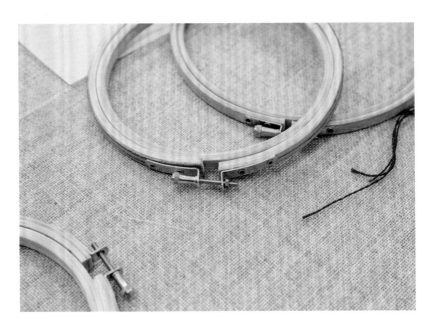

▲ Using embroidery hoops is optional so try working on your kantha with and without one, to see which way you prefer.

Threads

There are so many types of thread available in cotton, silk, linen, metallics and blends. There are no rules for choosing threads; the only criteria is how well they help you translate your ideas onto cloth. Before committing to a thread type or number of strands in your kantha, I suggest that you experiment and explore widely – try wool yarn, silk and linen threads and discover what you resonate with. Allow yourself to be surprised and always make a note of the shade number and brand in your sketchbook, along with a small length so you can reorder if you run out mid-project.

Cotton floss threads are excellent for kantha embroidery as you can use a varying number of strands to achieve a variety of weights of line. Cotton perle no. 8 is a good option for quilting as it offers a different kind of mark and is more robust compared to two or three strands of floss. I use both floss and perle for embroidery and quilting because of the variation in marks I can achieve.

◀ Use different thread types. Play with contrast – place a thick thread next to a thin one or a shiny thread next to a matt one – and watch your art come alive.

◀ Perle threads are a good option for quilting.

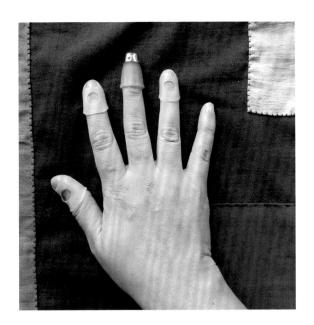 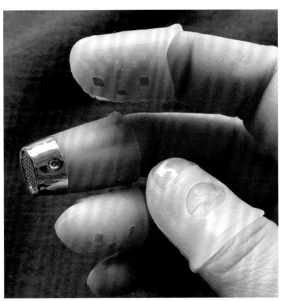

◄ Thimbles and needle pullers.

Other Useful Tools

Embroidery Scissors

A sharp pair of embroidery scissors is essential in your tool kit. They help in clipping threads and allow you to get close to the surface of the fabric. I use a pair of stork scissors.

Needle Threader

Needle threaders are helpful in getting the thread through the eye of the needle swiftly. I recommend that you invest in one.

Heat-erasable Pens

I use heat-erasable pens in sizes 0.5 and 0.7 to transfer drawings onto fabric. After completion, the drawing can be removed easily by ironing over it or introducing warm air with a hairdryer. Occasionally, the marks can come back at low temperatures, so do bear that in mind if using these pens.

Thimbles & Needle Pullers

Good-quality thimbles and needle pullers can make a big difference in stitching comfortably over extended periods. There are several types of thimbles available in metal, leather and silicone. Try them out to find which one suits you best.

Embroidery & Quilting

Embroidery and quilting offer endless creative possibilities as both encourage you to create different types of marks and texture on the cloth. Start by selecting the stitches you wish to use and test them on your chosen fabrics. I find it helpful to outline a general plan for stitch techniques in my sketchbook, treating it as a flexible roadmap rather than a rigid recipe.

Allow the stitches to engage in a conversation with your composition, the ground cloth and threads, and let the work develop from there. Embrace the freedom to change and improvise as needed, letting your embroidery evolve organically. Once the embroidery is completed, be aware that the surface will change again after the quilting is done.

To create dynamic compositions, incorporate contrast into your embroidery. There are various ways to achieve this:

∾ **Texture:** Experiment with the interplay of thick and thin yarns, adding dimension and tactile interest to your piece.

∾ **Weight of stitch line:** Vary the number of floss strands you use to produce a range of line weights. This technique adds depth and visual impact to your embroidery.

∾ **Length of stitch:** Play with different stitch lengths to build sections with short stitches for intricate details and others with longer stitches for bold accents. This variation adds rhythm and visual appeal to your design.

∾ **Scale:** Combine small and large motifs in your composition, creating an intriguing contrast that draws the viewer's attention and adds visual interest.

∾ **Colour:** Explore value contrast by pairing dark and light tones. This technique enhances the depth and visual dynamics of your embroidery.

You don't need to incorporate all of these contrast elements in a single piece; instead choose one or two to focus on and experiment with.

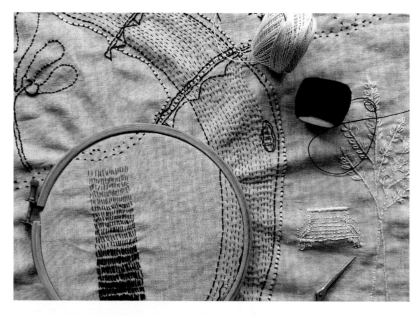

▲ Following the needle's journey across the cloth is part of my meditative practice. It gives me the space to quietly focus and reflect on everyday experiences, and come to a place of equanimity.

◄ Turn your needle around so an embroidered motif is not distorted by quilting.

Tips for Embroidery & Quilting

ᔐ Thread several needles before you begin to embroider, so you do not have to stop to rethread every so often.

ᔐ Begin your embroidery from the centre and gradually work your way outwards, allowing your design to unfold and take shape with each stitch.

ᔐ Using a varying number of floss strands can enable you to achieve a variety of marks.

ᔐ Protect your fingers – invest in good-quality thimbles and needle pullers. I use a metal-tip silicone thimble and silicone needle pullers that enable me to stitch comfortably for hours.

ᔐ Consider how the quilting will impact your embroidered design. The quilting and embroidery stitches need to complement one another. To keep my embroidered image intact, I often do not quilt over my motifs.

ᔐ Do not worry about knots being visible. Knots are simply a way of grounding your thread into the fabric – as important as the stitch itself. If you are making a reversible piece, then replace knots with a small back stitch to begin and end your stitch.

ᔐ Use different thread types and thicknesses to make your embroidered art more dynamic. Think of these as your paintbrushes – each will give you a different mark.

ᔐ Approach kantha making as creative play. Experiment with forms, colours, scale and composition.

ᔐ Don't be afraid to take risks – push yourself out of your comfort zone and try new things. Pay attention to what you enjoy creating and what resonates with you, and do more of it.

▲ Varying the number of floss strands can enable you to achieve different weights of line.

▲ Use different thread types and thicknesses to make your embroidered art more dynamic.

Finishing

Edges

Once the embroidery and quilting are completed, trim all excess threads and tails with a sharp pair of embroidery scissors and square off your corners using a set square.

How you finish off your edges will depend on the display you have in mind. If raw edges are important to you, simply leave them visible. If you prefer to not have raw edges visible, you could turn the edges inside a knife fold and finish with a blanket stitch or, alternatively, turn seam allowances over to the reverse of the piece and finish off with simple hemming. Another option is finishing with a bias binding or turning the backing over to the front.

Ironing

Lay a soft towel or blanket on your ironing table and then place your kantha face down over it for ironing. Always iron from the reverse so the embroidery stays intact. If you need to iron the front, keep a scrap piece of fabric over it to ensure no errant steam marks or heat stains mark your kantha. The heat will remove any drawing, so iron only at the end when all the embroidery and quilting has been completed.

Sign Your Work

So many beautiful works of kantha art are anonymous. I feel sad to see these orphaned pieces, so I urge you to sign your work by stitching your name either on the front or the reverse of your piece. You can use back stitches or running stitches for your signature. Consider adding a date – it is so useful in tracing how your work has developed over time.

◀ Square off your corners and cut extra seam allowance away.

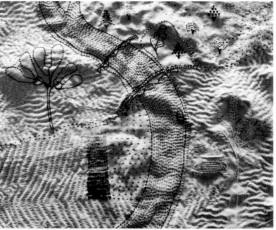

◀ As a general rule, try to retain as much of the texture as possible; tactility is such a distinctive quality of kantha.

◀ I embroider my signature on the front using a combination of straight and back stitches.

Display

There are several options for displaying kantha. Traditional kantha were intended to be viewed laid flat from all sides, therefore the orientation of motifs was intentionally kept non-directional. However, this need not be the case today. Choose the display method that resonates with your style and complements the qualities you wish to enhance. Here are some suggestions for displaying your kantha on the wall:

Unstretched & Framed

Place your kantha in a floating frame to maintain its organic form and tactile quality. Attach it to the background with small stitches or acid-free tape. This approach allows you to showcase the edges and retain more of the sculptural texture.

Stretched & Framed

For a more structured display, stretching your kantha over a mountboard is an ideal option. Secure the corners neatly with staples or stitches, ensuring a smooth, taut surface. It's worth noting that this method may slightly flatten the texture and result in folded edges. You can choose to frame the kantha behind glass or leave it uncovered, depending on your preference and the overall aesthetic you desire.

Unstretched & Unframed

If you prefer a more relaxed and natural presentation, consider the unstretched and unframed method. Attach a fabric sleeve along the top and bottom edges of your kantha on the reverse side. This sleeve allows you to hang and display your kantha using various items, such as an elegant branch, a wooden dowel, a bamboo pole or even an extendable curtain pole. This approach adds an organic and effortless charm to your kantha display.

Conclusion

In an era of increasing busyness and dwindling attention spans, as landfills overflow and our planet's resources diminish, kantha invites us to pause, to inhabit our bodies and lives more fully, to be more thoughtful to our planet and to express ourselves with greater courage.

Kantha embodies multilayered meanings within its folds: self-expression, identity, comfort, memories, empowerment, mindfulness, connection and sustainability. I hope our exploration of these strands in the preceding chapters, along with kantha's history and a lexicon of its stitches, has inspired you and brought you closer to this remarkable tradition. Kantha does not belong in museums simply to be admired for its superlative needlework; it is a philosophy, a way of life that can offer us many tools for future making.

Kantha is the assertion of individual agency and a reminder that creativity thrives despite constraints – in fact, it presents evidence to the contrary that creativity thrives because of constraints. Kantha urges us to not wait for perfect materials, for every conceivable thread colour or for inspiration to strike before we decide to stitch, but rather to just begin with what we have and harness those constraints to find creative solutions.

In today's dizzyingly busy world, where our experiences are increasing fractured by screens and algorithms, kantha are tactile invitations to slow down and be more connected to our bodies and our minds. Through thoughtful acts of mending and repurposing cloth, inspired by the spirit of kantha we can create a future that is kinder to our planet.

Rozsika Parker noted in *The Subversive Stitch* that she 'identified the historical hierarchical division of the arts into fine arts and craft as a major force in the marginalisation of women's work.' By challenging such antiquated hierarchies, we honour the artistic women whose needlework has thus far remained outside what was recognised as art, and we push open the door a little wider for those who are yet to come.

As we conclude this transformative journey, I hope it marks the beginning of a new path for you – one that leads to fulfilment, joy in personal expression, solace in connecting with your inner self and a sense of camaraderie with others on a similar quest. May your continued exploration bring you closer to finding your own creative fulfilment and deepen your connection to the world around you.

Suppliers

Medium & Lightweight Linen & Cotton

UK

Cloth House London: clothhouse.com

Flax Mill Textiles: flaxmill.eu

Merchant & Mills: merchantandmills.com

WBL Fabrics: whaleys-bradford.ltd.uk

US

Amazon Fabric: fabric.com

Dharma Trading Co.: dharmatrading.com/
fabric/fabric-from-dharma-trading-co.html

Fabrics-Store.com: fabrics-store.com

Robert Kaufman Fabrics: robertkaufman.com

Threads

Au Ver à Soie: boutiqueproavas.com

DMC: dmc.com

Valdani: valdani.com

Wonderfil Specialty Threads: wonderfil.co.uk
(UK); shopwonderfil.com (US)

Haberdasheries

Sajou (Paris): sajou.fr/en

Liberty: libertylondon.com

Loop London: loopknitting.com

Needles & Accessories

Quilting Needles

Clover: clover-mfg.com/product/6/241

Embroidery Needles

Clover: clover-mfg.com/product/6/245

Prym: prym.com/en/crewel-needles-
424#product-detail-variant

Milliners Needles

Clover: clover-mfg.com/product/6/252

Silicone Thimble with Metal Tip

Clover: clover-mfg.com/product/9/260

Silicone Needle Pullers

Prym: prym.com/en/needle-grabber-271

Embroidery Hoops

Elbesee Products: elbesee.co.uk

Pilot Frixion Heat-erasable Pens

Medium Tip (0.7): pilotpen.co.uk/en/collections/
must-have/frixion-family/frixion-ball-clicker-0-7-
gel-ink-rollerball-pen-medium-tip.html

Fine Tip (0.5): pilotpen.co.uk/en/collections/
must-have/frixion-family/frixion-point-clicker-0-
5-gel-ink-rollerball-pen-fine-tip.html

A4 Light Box

Amazon: amzn.eu/d/3INiL7P

Acknowledgements

This book would not have been possible without the support of so many individuals and institutions, family and friends. I would like to thank my publishers for inviting me to write this book and to my editors Clare Martelli and Natasha Collin for their unwavering support.

In Delhi, gratitude to Nidhi Kamra at the National Crafts Museum, and her team, including Sundarji, for their assistance in studying and photographing the museum's kantha collection. Special thanks to Neeru Kumar for access to her kantha collection and to David Abraham for his insights which greatly enriched my research.

In Ahmedabad, my appreciation goes to Lalitha Poluru and the entire staff at the Knowledge Management Centre at NID Ahmedabad. Special thanks to Asha and Suhrid Sarabhai, and the staff at the Sarabhai Foundation, Calico Museum of Textiles for granting access to the library and museum. Heartfelt thanks to my friend and fellow artist Nehal Desai for her hospitality and kindness.

In Bangalore, heartfelt thanks to my mentor, Aditi Ranjan, for her wisdom and guidance, and to my friend Kavita Arvind, for her hospitality and company on research trips. To Anitha Reddy for insights on Kawandi quilts, and Dipak Jain for access to his kantha collection. To Abhishek Poddar and Vaishnavi Kambadur at the Museum of Art and Photography (MAP) Bengaluru for their support in studying kantha archives at MAP.

In Kolkata, I am particularly grateful to Aditi Roy Ghatak for her warm-hearted hospitality, unending kindness and for opening many doors that would have remained closed otherwise. Special thanks to Ruby Palchoudhari and everyone at Crafts Council of West Bengal and Birla Academy of Art & Culture. Thanks to the staff and curatorial team, especially Sankha Basu at The Ramakrishna Mission Institute of Culture, Kolkata; and to Mahua Lahiri and Pritikana Goswami, Aloke Kumar, Mahamaya Sikdar, Rituparna Ghosh for their generous sharing of knowledge and expertise. My appreciation to Rupa Mehta and Swagata Ghosh at SASHA; Bappaditya Biswas at Byloom; Malika Verma and Shamlu Dudeja at SHE Kantha; Darshan Shah at Weavers Studio Kolkata; Priyanka Raja at Experimenter and Ratna Basu for access to their collections and insights.

In Katna, my sincere thanks to Shabnam Ramaswamy for her hospitality in Murshidabad, and for providing access to the Street Survivors India kantha archives. Her insights, and the discussions and demonstrations she arranged with kantha makers, especially Mohila and Tumpa, have immensely enriched my research. To Rajiv Gautam for his invaluable feedback, photographs, and assistance during and after my visit to West Bengal. My gratitude to the members of Street Survivors India for sharing their expertise in kantha making.

In North America, my thanks to Darielle Mason at the Philadelphia Museum of Art, Pika Ghosh at Haverford College and Cathy Stevulak at The Threads for their insights.

I am deeply grateful to all the contributing artists and makers whose work I have been privileged to include in this book. A special mention to Katie Treggiden for her thought-provoking contribution, and to Raquel Calado for her assistance with stitching and photographing kantha techniques samples.

Thanks to photographers Yeshen Venema in London and Syed Asghar in Delhi for their sensitive work.

I am profoundly grateful to my family for their unwavering love and support: Divya, Anoop, Krishan, Puneet, Anju, and in particular my brother-in-law Mayank Mansingh Kaul who shared invaluable insights, resources and unfailingly pointed me in the right direction; and to my mother, whose memory continues to inspire me daily. I am grateful to my friends Shilpi Burman, Kavita Arvind, Vallari Harshwal, Anirban Dutta Gupta, Aditi Prakash, Nehal Desai, Sucharita Beniwal, Anuj Sharma, Rajeshwari Sengupta, Juhi Pandey for their support. Thanks to Pushkar Thakur for his camera and offering helpful insights on photography on field trips.

A special thanks to my children, Kabir and Kaavya, and my husband, Aditya, for being my biggest cheerleaders and the wind under my wings.

Picture Credits

All photography by the author, unless otherwise credited.

p.6: **Stitch by Stitch**.

p. 12: courtesy of **Crafts Council of West Bengal, Artisana store, Kolkata**.

pp. 13, 24, 25, 28, 29, 31, 32, 33 (both), 34 (top), 35 (bottom row), 36 (top and left), 38, 44–6, 49 (top), 52 (top), 54 (top), 56, 58, 60, 64 (top), 65 (top), 67, 75 (top), 76 (top), 82 (top), 84–5, 107 (top right, bottom left), 111, 118 (middle, bottom), 122, 123 (top and left): **collection of the National Crafts Museum and Hastkala Academy, New Delhi**. Photo: Syed Asghar.

p. 14: **collection of Prof. Aloke Kumar, Kolkata**. Photo: Rohan Chakravarty, Quarter Melon Studio.

pp. 15, 16, 70 (top), 71, 72 (top), 125, 135: **Yeshen Venema**.

p. 17 (all): **Kaushik Ramaswamy**.

pp. 26, 34 (bottom row), 35 (top), 36 (right), 61, 62 (top), 79, 87, 88 (both), 90–1, 96, 107 (bottom right), 115, 116 (both), 117: courtesy of **Street Survivors India, Katna, Murshidabad**. www.streetsurvivorsindia.in

pp. 37 (bottom), 123: **David Abraham**.

pp. 39, 105 (right): collection of **The Museum and Art Gallery, The Ramakrishna Mission Institute of Culture, Gol Park, Kolkata**.

pp. 98–9: **Rajiv Gautam**.

pp. 126 (top), 127: **Laura Berman**.

p. 126 (bottom): **Lesli Michaelis Onusko**.

p. 137 (bottom row) **Adele Annette**.

pp. 140 (both), 142, 143: **Jhaveri Contemporary**.

pp. 154, 155 (bottom): **David Bennett**.

p. 156: **Mary Stark**.

p. 161: **Saurabh Behar**.

p. 162 (both): **Priyanka Chabbra**.

p. 163 (both): **Pranoy Sarkar**.

p. 166 (top): **Ankita Roy**.

p. 168: **Lavina Baldota**.

Front cover (clockwise): **collection of the National Crafts Museum and Hastkala Academy, New Delhi**. Photo: Syed Asghar; photo: **Ekta Kaul**; photo: **Yeshen Venema**.

Back cover: photo: **Ekta Kaul**.

Spine: photo: **Yeshen Venema**.

Bibliography

Ahmad, Perveen, *The Aesthetics & Vocabulary of Nakshi Kantha (Bangladesh National Museum Collection)*, Bangladesh National Museum, Bangladesh 1997

Bandyopadhyay, Romi, *Nakshi Kanthas of Bangladesh* [Craft Documentation], National Institute of Design, Ahmedabad, 2008

Basu, Rituparna, 'The History of Kantha Art', *The Journal of Women's Studies*, vol. 3:1–2, 1999

Chakrabarti, Asis K., *Kantha: The Traditional Art of the Women of Bengal*, Arts India Publications, Kolkata, 2000

Colton, Virginia, ed., *Reader's Digest Complete Guide to Needlework*, The Reader's Digest Association, Inc., White Plains, NY, 1979

Finn, Patrick J., *Quilts of India: Timeless Textiles*, Niyogi Books, New Delhi, 2014

Ghosh, Pika, *Making Kantha, Making Home: Women at Work in Colonial Bengal*, University of Washington Press, Seattle, WA, 2020

Gillow, John, et al., *Kantha*, Radius Books/Mingei International Museum, Santa Fe, NM, 2017

Haque, Enamul, *Woven Air: Muslin and Kantha Tradition of Bangladesh*, Whitechapel Art Gallery, London, 1988

Mason, Darielle, *Kantha: The Embroidered Quilts of Bengal*, Philadelphia Museum of Art, Philadelphia, PA, 2009

Morrell, Anne, *The Techniques of Indian Embroidery*, Interweave Press, Golden, CO, 1995

Parker, Roszika, *The Subversive Stitch: Embroidery and the Making of the Feminine*, Bloomsbury Visual Arts, London, 2019

Senapati, Arnab, *Living Tradition of Katna's Kantha: Practice of Kantha Making in Murshidabad District, West Bengal* [Craft Documentation], National Institute of Design, Ahmedabad, 2008

Tagore, Abanindranath and Stella Kramrisch, eds, 'Kantha', *Journal of the Indian Society of Oriental Art*, 7, 1939

Uddin, Jasim, *The Field of the Embroidered Quilt: A Tale of Two Indian Villages*, Oxford University Press, Oxford, 1939

Zaman, Niaz, *The Art of Kantha Embroidery*, University Press Ltd, Bangladesh, 1995

www.gardnermuseum.org/blog/connecting-cultural-worlds-embroidery-india-celebrating-portugals-monarchy

www.thenatureofcities.com/2016/05/26/sense-of-place

Index of Stitch Techniques

Knots   41–3

Quilter's   41

Finishing   42–3

Outline stitches   46–65

Running   46–7

Darning   48

Double darning/running   49–50

Back   51

Stem   52–3

Chain   54–5

Cable   56–7

Split   58–9

Fly   60–1

Mala (or double chain)   62–3

Herringbone   64

Cross   65

Filling stitches   66–83

Pattern darning   66–7

Filling pattern darning   68–9

Stripe pattern darning   70–1

Chevron pattern darning   72–3

Circular pattern darning: spiral motif   74

Circular pattern darning: wheel motif   75

Grid pattern darning   76

Bending stitch/diagonal bands
pattern darning   77

Convent stitch/Bokhara couching   78–80

Fishbone stitch   81

Jali stitch   82–3

Geometric   86–99

Pattern darning combination   86

Running stitch and detached chain
stitch combinations   87–9

Examples of motifs and patterns   90–1

Holbein stitch   92–4

Interlaced running stitch   95–9

Botanical   100–2

Popular motifs   102

Kadam phool   102

Border stitches   104–5

Quilting stitches   106–9

Kantha stitch   106–9